THE PARTNERSHIP WAY

The

NEW TOOLS FOR LIVING & LEARNING:
A Practical Companion for
The Chalice and the Blade

Healing Our Families,
Our Communities,
and Our World

Partnership Way

Riane Eisler

David Loye

 HarperSanFrancisco

A Division of HarperCollins*Publishers*

Many of the illustrations in this book have been copied from ancient works of art found by archeologists in prehistoric sites. Others are original works. As in both cases the line drawings are the work of contemporary artists, they are so credited at the end of each caption.

Library of Congress Cataloging-in-Publication Data
Eisler, Riane Tennenhaus.
    The partnership way : new tools for living and learning : a practical companion for the Chalice and the blade in our lives, our communities, and our world / Riane Eisler, David Loye.
      p.   cm.
    ISBN 0–06–250290–5
    1. Sex role. 2. Social skills. 3. Life skills. I. Loye, David.
II. Title.
HQ1075.E58   1990
305.3—dc20   89–45956
                                             CIP

98 97 96 95   RRD(H)   9 8 7 6 5

As the Acknowledgments show, putting together this book has
been a real partnership, not only between the coauthors
but with many other creative and dedicated women and
men. Therefore, we want to dedicate this book to all the
wonderful people who have given so much of their time
and energy because they believe
The Partnership Way can really make a difference.

Contents

Welcome to
The Partnership Way!

Welcome to *The Partnership Way.* We hope you will find it a helpful guide to an exciting and enjoyable journey through both the rapids and the shoals of contemporary personal and social change.

The Partnership Way is intended to probe more deeply the choices before us, to help us create more satisfying, more meaningful, less tense, less hurtful, and just plain healthier and more enjoyable options both for our daily lives and our planet.

For a long time many of us have been aware of something basically wrong in our lives, but have found it extremely difficult to do much about it since we could not even name it or clearly visualize another way of being. Indeed, most of what has been taught to us as history seemed to indicate that there is no other way. That has been the underlying assumption, and we all tend to take our basic assumptions for granted, no matter how limiting and destructive they may be.

The Chalice and the Blade: Our History, Our Future by Riane Eisler takes us back to a time before these assumptions became embedded in our psyches and our culture, a time now being reconstructed through a veritable archeological revolution. It shows us that there *is* an alternative: another way of living, of loving, and of creating a world that is both safe and exciting.

The Partnership Way was created for all those who want to explore these ideas and the information presented in *The Chalice and the Blade* in more depth. In fact, it was created in response to an outpouring of requests from people who have already formed discussion groups to study *The Chalice and the Blade* and its implications for healing ourselves and the world, as well as from university, college, and high school teachers who are using the book in their classes.

We know that to heal ourselves we have to understand what lies behind our symptoms and that this understanding is a prerequisite for any real change. Above all, we have to believe that change is not only desirable, but also possible. And this belief that a healthy alternative exists has to penetrate our unconscious minds, not just on the *intellectual* but also on the deeper *emotional* level to enable us to take appropriate action.

This is why *The Partnership Way* is not only a guide to deeper thought and discussion; it also provides opportunities for both imagining and experiencing different ways of thinking and feeling. Even beyond that, it offers suggestions for action, for ways to help accelerate the shift from a dominator to a partnership way of life.

Like *The Chalice and the Blade, The Partnership Way* takes us into uncharted territory. It takes us on a new, and at the same time very ancient, path. It is a path of exploration and adventure, a path that is still very much in the making.

We have put together some of the guideposts for this path out of our experience and we have set them forth in the pages that follow. But the actual construction of the path, the specific materials and the labor, will come from *your* experiences. And it is *you* who will make the journey your own.

The Partnership Way is your personal guide. You will find in it room to write down your own thoughts and feelings. Because you will probably use it as a guide for groups, it has been designed to facilitate the sharing of your ideas, feelings, and experiences. And since many people worked together in writing this book, we invite you to join us in this participatory process of creation. Please send us your impressions, suggestions, and action-oriented ideas. Strengthening and improving *The Partnership Way* will be a continuing project, a joint challenge and adventure for us all.

Riane Eisler and David Loye

THE PARTNERSHIP
PERSPECTIVE

These partners with chalice are from a vase in the Museum of Naples dating from the middle of the sixth century. The male is the god Dionysus, the female the goddess Semele. The chalice is Dionysus' characteristic high-handled wine cup, the *Kantharos*. They are surrounded by the ripe wine grapes of Semele. Line drawing from original: John Mason.

How to Use
The Partnership Way

The Partnership Way is a tool for rethinking and restructuring our lives. It is designed to help us clear the ground of old deadwood that impedes our way and put together some of the personal and social building blocks for a more balanced future for ourselves and our children: a world modeled on partnership rather than domination.

The Partnership Way is divided into three parts: The Partnership Perspective, The Partnership Study Guide, and Partnership Resources. Specific guidelines for use are given in each of these parts.

There is still another part, which is yours to create: *The Partnership Way* Personal Journal. We have designed this book with wide margins so you can easily make notes and comments as you read quotes, cartoons, drawings and pictures, songs, names of books and articles, and so on. In other words, you can create your own partnership resource directory. As you meet with others, you can share these resources to the benefit of all.

THE PARTNERSHIP PERSPECTIVE

The Partnership Perspective summarizes the differences between the dominator model and the partnership model, and suggests ways to facilitate partnership discussion and study by groups. It has sections on facilitating and communications, as well as on use for colleges, high schools, religious institutions, and recovery groups.

5

THE PARTNERSHIP STUDY GUIDE

The Partnership Study Guide is designed for use by either experienced or first-time facilitators. For those who want to proceed with a minimum of planning and start-up time, the study guide offers a session-by-session plan. Others will want to construct their own plan, drawing from all the materials in this book.

The Partnership Study Guide outlines nine sessions designed for use by community, church, self-help, and other groups. It can also be adapted for college and high school courses.

Those who want to create their own study guide may want to combine selections from the nine sessions with material presented in the second section of the *Study Guide*, called Additional Exercises and Topics for Discussion, as well as from the *Partnership Resources*.

PARTNERSHIP RESOURCES

Partnership Resources is a mix of new conceptual information and practical action-oriented tools, focusing on subjects ranging from the family and human rights to language and technology. It offers materials to supplement the nine session series or as an additional resource for those people who want to design their own plan.

We think you will enjoy **The Partnership Way**. It integrates both work and play, both left and right brain, both logic and imagination, both ritual and everyday practically, both the secular and the spiritual. It has been fun for us to put it together. We hope you will have fun using it.

This depiction of a killing from horseback, based on a Greco-Roman votive relief, shows the dramatic shift in the content of art that comes with the dominator shift in prehistory. Gone is the celebration of nature, love, and life. Now the artist, both as a matter of depicting the changed reality and because this is what "sells," must celebrate destruction, hate, and death. Line drawing from the original: John Mason.

By contrast are these Etruscan figures, woman and man, showing real affection. Etruscan art, though now also celebrating death and destruction, still shows a strong relationship to the earlier time and the art of Minoan Crete. These partners were immortalized in the terracotta of their sarcophagus in Cerveteri, Italy, about 520 B.C. Line drawing from the original: John Mason.

From Domination to Partnership

What is a dominator society? And what do we mean by partnership?

Most of us are quite familiar with what *The Chalice and the Blade* identifies as the dominator model. We may not have called it that or seen how its various elements relate to one another, but we have certainly experienced the pain, fear, and tension that come from a way of living based on physical or psychological control.

Such control is part of the dominator model. This model lies at the root of both war and the war of the sexes, both wife beating and child beating, both the exploitation and rape of other humans and of nature.

It is the model that many women and men are today questioning as they reexamine the conventional assumptions about the necessity for war, the ravages of "man's conquest of nature," and the "dysfunctional family" with its stereotypical female and male roles of domination and submission that have caused so much tension, loneliness, and pain.

The partnership model is somewhat harder for us to identify, because we have only experienced it in bits and pieces, in fleeting glimpses of what it might be like to live a different way. We have had few guidelines for living in partnership through our schools and universities or our art, books, and other media.

The term *partnership* itself is a good example. Because we need terms to describe a larger system of social interaction based on links founded on mutuality rather than chains of domination and subservience, we have chosen this term, even though until now it has been primarily used to refer to a business agreement or a marriage contract.

On the social level, partnership is the alternative to *both* patriarchy and matriarchy. On the personal level, all interactions have the possibility of partnership, because interaction based on mutual respect and empowerment, which is the essence of the partnership model, can happen with all kinds of people in all kinds of different settings.

Partnership can be between a woman and a man or between a number of women and/or men. It can be between women and women, men and men, parents and children. It can be between organizations, communities, and nations. It can even be with ourselves, as when we decide that we are going to do everything we can to live in harmony with our bodies and minds. And if we treat nature with respect, recognizing our interconnectedness with our natural habitat, that too is a way of living in partnership.

The basic configurations and key characteristics of the partnership and dominator models are detailed in the Charts and Graphs on pp. 179–90. The readings from *The Chalice and the Blade* assigned in each of the nine sessions outlined in the study guide provide an in-depth view of these two models and how they affect every area of society. And the pages that follow are designed to deepen and solidify this understanding so that we can more effectively identify, strengthen, develop, and disseminate principles and habits of partnership in all aspects of our lives.

The female figure is from a group of three women, probably priestesses, known as "the Blue Ladies." The male figure is known either as "the Young Prince" or "the Priest King." They date back to 1600 B.C. and can both be seen at the Palace in Knossos, Crete. Particularly fascinating is the Minoan feeling for light-hearted, high-style fashions these figures display. Line drawings from the originals: Jeff Helwig.

The Partnership Way
for Group Facilitators
and Teachers

Facilitator is a new word for leader. It describes a way of leading appropriate for a partnership rather than a dominator world.

The conventional definition of a leader—the one we have been taught in our schools, where we learn about famous generals, emperors, and kings—is that a leader is a man who gives orders, who controls others. Today, as we are trying to shift from a dominator to a partnership society, this old "strong-man" model of leadership is being challenged.

In both the political and corporate worlds we are hearing more and more about a new kind of leader or manager. This is someone—a woman or a man—who inspires rather than commands, who brings forth the best in others rather than cowing them into submission; someone who elicits creativity and trust rather than rote obedience and fear. Clearly, this is a style of leadership suitable for a partnership rather than a dominator society.

The partnership way for leaders is still largely uncharted territory. We simply have not been taught how to lead in partnership. Quite the contrary, in popular parlance we still speak of "leaders" and "followers." But not so long ago, people thought (and acted) in terms of "rulers" and "subjects." We have already come a long way.

Today there is a growing literature on new styles of collaborative leadership. There is also a growing tendency to see a group leader as a facilitator who makes it easier and more fun for people to work in groups.

12

The guidelines that follow are primarily designed for those who do not have facilitator experience. But we think they will help all facilitators to more easily and enjoyably organize and facilitate partnership study groups.*

FORMING AND NURTURING A PARTNERSHIP GROUP

To form a partnership group, a good way to start is to talk about *The Chalice and the Blade* with friends and neighbors, at school, work, church, or wherever you meet. You may want to ask people if they would like to meet in what is essentially a wellness rather than a therapy group: an exploration of more productive and satisfying thought, feeling, and action.

An effective study group can vary in size from two to as many as thirty or even forty people. But if you have a large group, dividing it into smaller units, as outlined in the material that follows, is very important.

There is no guaranteed process by which a facilitator and a group create an environment that is supportive, open, and growth-producing. There are processes, however, that have been used effectively by group facilitators in a variety of settings, and we share those processes here. Experienced facilitators will be familiar with those listed and may add others. We share these guidelines out of our collective experience in the hope that they will be helpful to you.

Choosing the Facilitators

Because working in partnership is the central theme of *The Partnership Way,* we strongly recommend choosing two cofacilitators. And because partnership between the female and male halves of humanity is the foundation for a partnership society, we suggest that the cofacilitators for groups that include both women and men be a woman and a man.

These two cofacilitators may be the original organizers. Or they may be chosen at the first meeting. Or the group may want to choose different facilitators for different sessions. In that event, it is essential for continuity and smooth functioning that two people take responsibility for overall administration.

*We gratefully acknowledge that some of our guidelines are adapted and excerpted from the excellent Guidelines for Leaders in *Cakes for the Queen of Heaven,* and we thank both its author, Shirley Ranck, as well as its publisher, the Unitarian Universalist Association, for permission to use them.

Creating the Partnership Environment

Working in partnership, the cofacilitators are responsible for finding a location and creating an environment conducive to partnership interaction. You may have to alternate locations, but for continuity it is better to find a place that can be used throughout the sessions.

Try to arrange for a comfortable, attractive meeting space appropriate to the size of the group. The physical setting can contribute greatly to harmonious interaction among participants. If change in the meeting place becomes necessary, be sure to let the group know well in advance.

Try to work in a circle and use a space large enough to make this possible. This way everyone can see everyone else and partnership is more easily facilitated.

Supplies and Other Resources

You will need a number of basic supplies for each meeting. These include at least two large newsprint pads and a number of large-point felt-tip pens (black and also some colors, for more effective presentations). The best way to use the newsprint pad is with an easel, as this ensures easy visibility for the whole group. You should also have some masking tape in case you want to put up sheets of newsprint for people to see their input. These supplies are easily obtained at art supply stores.

Other materials, such as visuals (books, artwork, photos, and slides) will help add richness to the meetings. Audio materials such as tapes may also be useful. (Tapes of Riane Eisler and others talking about related subjects are available through the Center for Partnership Studies.)

Where appropriate, the use of music at the beginning and the end of each session can do much to create a relaxed and open atmosphere. Not only the cofacilitators but also members of the group can take responsibility for selecting and bringing tapes and records as well as visual materials.

RESPONSIBILITIES OF THE COFACILITATORS

While every member of the group is an active partner, the cofacilitators have the primary responsibility for making this an enjoyable sharing and learning experience supportive of personal growth and positive social transformation.

To ensure this, it is important that you:

- Plan to be at all sessions. Continuity of leadership is important in building group cohesiveness. If you are cofacilitating and must be absent, let the group know in advance. Whenever a group facilitator is absent, interrelationships must be rebuilt.

- Plan to arrive before the other group members and have all equipment and materials ready for the session. This helps participants to feel comfortable and contributes to an organized, relaxed flow in the group process.

- Try to begin and end the sessions on time. Ask group members to let you know if they expect to be late or miss a session. Absences raise questions and concerns about the well-being of the missing person. A group does not function effectively if there are questions about a member's absence.

- Read through the outlines of the nine sessions before the series begins. Review each session's outline before the session begins. Being familiar with what is to be covered in the current and subsequent sessions will enable you to sense when you can go into a topic in more depth and when you will need to move on.

- Be prepared to write summary statements at the end of each session.

- Bring your copy of *The Chalice and the Blade* and ask the participants to bring their own copies to all meetings, as this makes it possible for people to find passages that have been of particular importance to them and share them with the group.

- Keep notes of what happens each time in the group: the kinds of experiences related, the insights learned, what seemed to excite the participants most. Use this information to help you plan later sessions and to remind the group from time to time of the journey they have been taking.

It is essential that notes of each session be kept and that provision be made for this in advance. This is an important supplement to the use of the newsprint pad to write down key words and ideas. These notes make it possible for participants to review the ground they have covered, and serve as the basis for suggestions for improvements and additions to future editions of *The Partnership Way*.

Working in partnership, the cofacilitators are also responsible for:

- checking that the meeting place is available and readied for each meeting
- getting names, addresses, and phone numbers of all participants
- making announcements and sending notices if necessary
- encouraging participation
- facilitating summaries and closures at the end of each session
- passing out participants' names, addresses, and phone numbers to group members.

We would also appreciate cofacilitators sending names and addresses of participants and any suggestions for *The Partnership Way* to the Center for Partnership Studies.

ENCOURAGING PARTICIPANT INVOLVEMENT

The Partnership Study Guide provides session plans for a nine-week series. These plans suggest many possibilities and will have to be adapted to the needs and wishes of the members of the group. It is a good idea to encourage group members to participate in planning from the beginning. Specifically, they can be encouraged to:

- lead their own opening and closing ceremonies
- create some of the activities
- contribute additional readings and other materials.

To the extent that each participant can take an active role in creating the study group, the experience of working in partnership will be greatly enhanced. During the sessions, participants can do the following:

- be responsible for opening, closing, and/or facilitating parts of sessions
- report on supplemental readings
- take notes
- bring poems, music, books, tapes, and other resources.

The variations are endless. The primary intent is to offer practice in *shared leadership*. Enjoy and be creative, open to the richness and surprises that shared leadership can offer.

FACILITATING EXPERIENTIAL LEARNING

Since real learning is not just intellectual, the study guide also suggests experiential exercises for each session, often in the form of guided visualizations. For participants to benefit from these exercises, the cofacilitators should give special attention to the following elements.

Relaxation

Participants should be helped to relax and open themselves to new ideas and experiences. One way to do this is to ask people to close their eyes and take three deep breaths (inhaling and exhaling slowly), and then for thirty seconds to a minute to simply observe their breathing along with any thoughts and feelings that come up. It is very important that the cofacilitators be centered and that they speak very slowly, as this in itself has a relaxing effect. In this and other ways, they themselves model and communicate an open and relaxed state, creating a relaxed and safe environment for the group.

Preparation

It is a good idea to write out notes for the guided visualization beforehand. In fact, for all but the most experienced facilitators, it may be best to script everything, including the opening and closing directions.

Opening

For example, to begin each guided visualization, the facilitator tells the participants that she or he (or another member of the group) will take them on a guided visualization. Ask them to find a comfortable position to sit in, paying attention to how their bodies feel; to close their eyes, take a deep breath, and relax their bodies. Then ask them to just observe their thoughts as they go by, allowing their minds to relax too, gradually emptying their minds. Tell them to keep breathing slowly and deeply and that they should take a few moments to do this. Then begin the guided visualization, once again making sure to speak very slowly.

Closing

At the end of the guided visualization, allow for a few moments for people to stay in touch with their feelings and the thoughts and images evoked by the experience. Then ask them in a soft voice to open their eyes, and perhaps to stretch, before sharing what they experienced.

Questions

Posing specific questions about participants' experiences during the exercise can help them formulate their thoughts to share with the group. The study guide suggests some questions to use.

Time for Sharing

The most important part of guided visualizations and other experiential exercises is the opportunity to share the feelings, thoughts, and images the experience has evoked. Each person needs adequate time—depending on the exercise, at least five minutes per person. *Therefore, in groups larger than six to seven people, it is essential that the group divide itself into smaller subgroups for this experiential work in order to make enough time for everyone.*

Dyads are the most effective subgroups for sharing. This is almost the only way to go for large groups, since the next step after the small group sharing is for the larger groups to reconvene so that at least some of the members can summarize their experiences for the larger group—and this clearly takes longer in larger groups. Where group size and time parameters make it possible, it is best if all participants can share their experiences with the larger group. A nice—and usually quicker—variation on this is to have each person's dyad partner summarize for the larger group what the other member shared with her or him.

It is essential that the cofacilitators communicate to the group that during experiential work, group members must truly listen to each other. This is not just a question of common courtesy; it is the basis for establishing a sense of belonging founded on mutual trust. To develop trust, group members must feel that everyone will be heard and will be reasonably safe from criticism. Trust is basically feeling that one is not being controlled, that even if someone does not like another person's opinion, he or she is willing to hear it.

Particularly in dyads doing experiential sharing, it is essential for the listener not to interrupt the speaker. This is something the cofacilitators should stress every time. And they should also encourage all the participants to work on their listening skills. (See also section on Partnership Communications.)

KEEPING IT GOING

Each group will have its own needs and preferences. Here are a few suggestions that facilitate group partnership process.

- Use the session plans flexibly; they are guides to adapt to the needs and preferences of the group. Encourage group members to express their suggestions for different formats or content. Try to maintain an even balance between activities and didactic input. It is usually a good rule of thumb to engage group members in exploring their present knowledge and feelings about an issue or topic before presenting new information.

- If your group is larger than six or seven, you may want to divide up into groups of two, three, or four for the discussion after the experiential work, with each group having a chance to report back to the whole on what they have discovered. This will ensure that everyone has a chance to be heard. At each session, members can work with a different group in order to experience the richness of the wisdom of all the participants, if everyone agrees to this.

- Try to know each member of your group, and help the group members get to know each other. Taking time to build group rapport and trust is an essential component of every session. It can be helpful at the beginning of each session to invite participants to tell of an experience of the past week that gave them new insight into how the partnership and dominator models affect our lives or to relate a personal observation they wish to share with the group.

- Respect each person's contribution or right to keep silent and remind the group to do likewise. Guarantee the right to pass. It is important for group rapport and trust that members not feel pressured into sharing more than they are ready to reveal.

- Strive to keep a single individual or small group from dominating the discussion. If this occurs, ask yourself what is happening. Has the topic released an issue of great concern? Are there individuals who feel threatened and are using this as a means to keep control? Uncovering a hidden agenda can be a key to new understanding.

- Help the group to keep focused. If individuals start to talk about other things, remind them of the subject or task, and make a note of their concern so that it can be addressed later or privately. Encourage group members to help you keep the focus. This can be a group responsibility.

- Be sure that insights and learnings arrived at by the group are gathered up and given expression, and that personal sharings are honored in some way. Provide a time in each session when this can be done or use the opening and closing ceremonies, where appropriate, to accomplish this purpose.

- Support group trust by having participants agree to keep personal confidences that have been shared within the group. No one wants her or his story retold elsewhere.

- Be sensitive to the potential emotional impact of this material on participants. Strong emotions may surface. Anger and rage may spring from unknown sources and mask pain. Tears and expressions of anger are clues to underlying strong emotions that people may have difficulty acknowledging and articulating. Give yourself and the other person time and room to express emotions. Make a decision about how to act when participants become emotional. Do not confuse support with agreement. You may support a person in her or his grief, fear, or anger, and be critical about what she or he does with it. Strong emotions are energy and as such can be channeled into constructive action. Ask questions, use your intuition, challenge assumptions, and make suggestions.

- Seek a balance in your own participation. This balance is dynamic. Encouraging others' participation is usually more fruitful than inadvertently being the one everyone turns to as the "expert."

- Take your time. Allow participants time to reflect at each session on their thoughts and experiences since the last meeting. Listen to the group and encourage clarification. Try to hear the questions behind the ones posed. Pay attention to new agenda items and interests.

PACING THE SESSIONS

The sessions will be more effective if the cofacilitators attend to and guide their pace.

Breaks

We all know that no matter how interesting a lecture or discussion may be, if it goes on too long, we tend to tune out. Since each session is designed to last several hours, adequate breaks are essential. Plan a ten- to fifteen-minute break at approximately the middle of each session. Be sure to schedule it at a natural breaking point, such as between the experiential work and the discussion.

Special Events

We all like to have something special to look forward to. So you may want to plan with the group to have a special event during the series—a potluck meal or informal party. This type of event works well close to the midpoint of the series. Plans need to be made, and if possible everyone should contribute something. It is important that someone coordinate this, and that a number of group members take responsibility for bringing all necessary equipment and food and/or making sure everyone who promised to bring something is clear on it and plans to follow through. It may also be nice to have some music for this session or some other way of making it special.

Those groups that cannot have a special meeting might want to make one of the sessions longer to provide time for some special refreshments, either after the meeting or during a longer midpoint break. This special event and the more informal party atmosphere are a good way to strengthen individual friendships as well as the feelings of belonging to a group, and to simply have some fun.

Closings

Instead of (or in addition to) a midpoint special event, group members might want to plan a meeting or party at or after the last session. If this is not possible, members may want to create a special closing ceremony for the final session. A special event or closing provides a sense of closure and accomplishment, and an opportunity to celebrate your shared experience and learnings and to say goodbye—or, even better, to make plans to continue meeting, either informally or as a group.

An ancient conversation. Based on a votive relief dedicated to Xenocrateia, fifth century B.C. Line drawing from the original: John Mason.

Partnership Communications

Though we have stressed communications in the preceding section, these skills are so generally essential *outside* as well as within discussion groups that we want to further focus on them here. In other words, we're thinking here of what helps build partnership in families, on the job, in schools, and everywhere else two or more of us are gathered.

Because the usual way of looking at communication is as a one-way street, as an act of imparting information to others, most of what we read about communication skills focuses on the communicator. But clearly it takes more than one to communicate. There is not only the writer but the reader, the receiver as well as the sender, the listener as well as the speaker.

In face-to-face personal communication, the role of the listener is critical. If we look at personal communication as a partnership where two or more people take turns talking and listening, we see that to build good relationships the listener's part is just as important as the speaker's. And if we recognize that good relationships are based on mutual trust, we also see that good listening skills are an essential ingredient.

Therefore, the communication guidelines that follow emphasize listening skills.

ACTIVE LISTENING

It is very important that people in a group truly listen to each other. For example, when working in dyads, a cardinal rule is that the speaker not be interrupted.

But listening is more than just not interrupting. It is acknowledging through one's active attention that the other person is being heard.

Perhaps most important is that people who are sharing their feelings be assured that they will not be criticized for having such feelings.

A very good way to ensure that you are truly listening to others—and that they *know* you are really listening—is to play back to them, in your own words, what you have just heard them say. You can say, for instance: "Let me see if I understand your point. You are saying that _____. Do I understand that correctly?"

While you put the other's views in your own words, it is important that you do not include any words or phrases that *evaluate* or *comment on* what the other person said. It should be a simple playback to be sure you heard and understood the point that was being made, whether or not you agree with it. The other person then has the opportunity to correct your impression if it was not quite accurate or complete. Once the understanding is achieved, the conversation can move on to comments, responses, or statements of other or additional views.

RESPECTFUL COMMUNICATIONS

When people are expressing opinions, it is of course important that others feel free to disagree and to say so. But there is such a thing as agreeing to disagree. And the key is not to make others feel that they are being controlled. In other words, people need to understand that even if others do not like their opinion, they are willing to hear it. That's what communication is about.

That is not to say that free communication means absolute freedom of speech. In both law and custom, there are essential limits, such as the prohibition against falsely yelling "Fire!" in a crowded theater or inciting violence against members of different racial or religious groups.

Free communication means respectful communication. And respectful communication is essential in partnership study groups, particularly during experiential work. Active listening needs to be encouraged and nurtured not only by the cofacilitators but by all members of the group as well.

These whimsical figures tell us much of both the Minoan Cretan sense of humor and—in marked contrast to what comes later—a comfortable, nonfearful attitude toward deity. They are from a Minoan plate found in the Old Palace of Phaistos, dating to 1800 B.C., that makes use of one of the many epiphanies of the Great Goddess, identified by Marija Gimbutas as the "Bee Goddess." In this case we have what seem to be two bee priestesses hovering about what appears to be the hive as Goddess. Line drawing from the original: Jeff Helwig.

The Partnership Way
for Colleges and
High Schools

Many college professors and high school teachers have adopted *The Chalice and the Blade* as an assigned or supplementary text for courses ranging from history, sociology, and women's studies to peace studies, futurism, and philosophy. Therefore, we have also designed *The Partnership Way* for use in these more formal settings.

The suggestions offered in this book can easily be integrated into a course plan prepared by the teacher, or they can be used as the basis for a section of the curriculum or for a whole course.

The Partnership Way is specifically designed to facilitate the integration of materials dealing with the history, analysis, problems, and aspirations of *both* women and men into the general curriculum. It is also useful as a basis for courses that focus on the social foundations of peace, particularly classes on Western civilization, women's studies, and peace studies. It provides materials to meet a variety of curriculum needs.

Teachers using *The Partnership Way* in a college course will find the Discussion Topics sections in the study guide most useful, as they offer a rich selection of questions for study and discussion. Teachers in high schools and some college courses will probably also want to use some of the experiential exercises described in the study guide. The Partnership Resources section provides additional materials for both students and teachers, including articles by Riane Eisler, charts on the partnership and dominator models, and other readings that students in classes ranging from English literature and current events to sociology, psychology, and women's studies will find useful.

26

For the teacher interested in helping students learn to live and work in partnership, *The Partnership Way* is an important resource not only because of its substantive content, but also because it integrates partnership ideas with actual participation in partnership process.

As teachers ourselves, we feel that one of the most important things we must teach children and young people is how to work in partnership. We have found a great hunger for such learning among students.

For example, when one of us taught a course at UCLA on the social and legal status of women, the students were asked to choose partners to work together on term projects for which they would be jointly responsible. It was an unusual course design, particularly for its time (1970), and some of the students were doubtful at first. But at the end of the course they almost unanimously endorsed this method. It was less tense, they said, than the usual one-against-one competitive mode. In fact, it was not only more enjoyable, but more effective. Most of the students said it had been a unique opportunity for them to exchange ideas with other students in a results-oriented way. *They could not understand why this was the only class they had ever taken that had actually helped them to work together in teams!*

Clearly, the lack of this kind of education for teamwork (except in highly competitive situations such as sports and debates) has caused many personal and social problems. It is also increasingly recognized as a source of major difficulties for the business and corporate sector, where teamwork is being found to yield far greater productivity and job satisfaction than the old mode of individual competition.

The tools offered in this book will not only aid teachers and others who want to help their students live and work in partnership, they will also provide the basis for a very important kind of research. This is what we call partnership research—a participatory action-oriented approach designed to identify, strengthen, and create partnership models for all aspects of our lives through group data gathering and testing.

We especially invite you and your students to contribute to this exciting new approach to research, teaching, and learning.

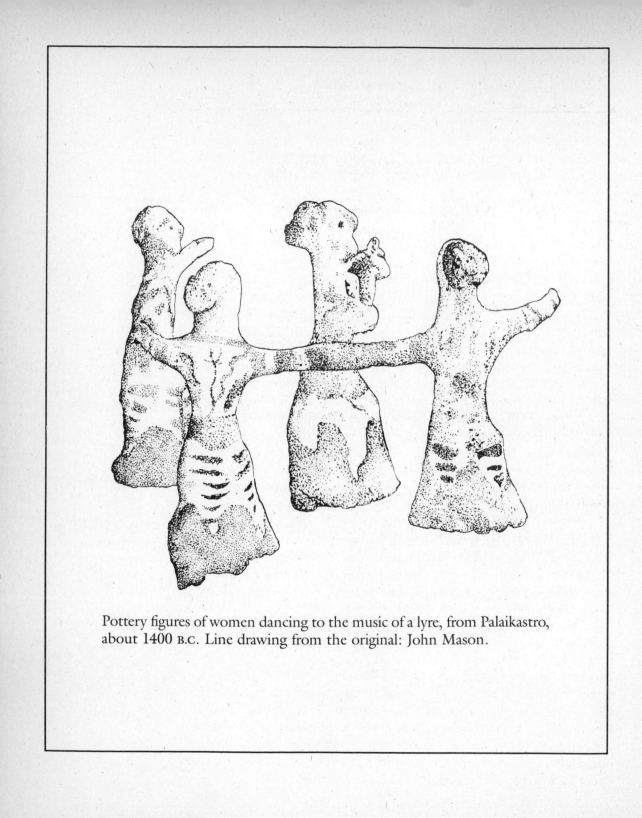

Pottery figures of women dancing to the music of a lyre, from Palaikastro, about 1400 B.C. Line drawing from the original: John Mason.

The Partnership Way for Religious Study or Independent Spiritual Development

While most major religions have at their core a partnership spirituality, they also have a dominator overlay. As a result, the essential message of our interconnectedness, powerfully expressed in the Jewish and Christian traditions by prophets like Joshua and by Jesus, has all too often been distorted in the way religion has been taught and practiced.

One of our most urgent tasks today is to strengthen the partnership core of religion. This book is designed to help us do this. It provides materials for individuals seeking a strong spiritual dimension in their lives as well as for religious study groups in the Catholic, Protestant, Jewish, Moslem, Hindu, and Buddhist traditions and congregations of the Church of Religious Science, Unitarian Universalists, Bahai'i, and others who combine teachings from all these traditions.

It is evident that we cannot build a true morality based on the subjugation of one half of humanity by the other. Partnership is an important tool for integrating and translating into action the "softer," more "feminine" teachings of most great religious and spiritual figures; it shows us how to do unto others as we would have them do unto us. Above all, it is a tool for the reintegration of spirituality into our lives, not as something we can only access through dogma from "higher up" but, as Jesus and many mystical teachers have taught, through *gnosis* or direct knowledge of the divinity in all aspects of life.

The partnership approach makes it possible for us to reclaim an important but still largely suppressed part of our religious history. For example, it allows both women and men to explore the Catholic veneration of the Virgin Mary as a continuation of ancient traditions where the deity was imaged as a Great Mother who had *both* divine daughters and sons. In Jewish tradition, it explains the presence of the female Shekina at the center of Hebrew mysticism. It also illuminates the centrality of "feminine" values such as caring, nonviolence, and compassion to the teachings of Jesus.

Most important, it offers us an integrated approach to our spiritual heritage. By providing a better understanding of our earliest forms of worship, it reconnects us with millennia-long traditions when the chalice—the power of love and illumination—was the governing image. And whether we are Jews or Christians, Hindus or Moslems, pagans, agnostics, or atheists, it helps us reclaim for ourselves and our children a more life-celebrating and life-enhancing kind of spirituality, firmly rooting it in a more just, harmonious, and ecologically balanced kind of society.

Because it is built on partnership between the female and male halves of humanity, a partnership spirituality supports the contemporary movement to reinstate women in religious leadership roles. At the same time, it reinstates the feminine in religious imagery and theology, greatly enriching both women's and men's spiritual lives. Indeed, by clarifying the partnership character of so-called "primitive Christianity," it brings many of the core ideas and practices of early Christianity back to life. And by providing us with new/old myths and images that recognize and honor the great spiritual potential of both women and men, it offers us a spirituality that gives new meaning and purpose to our lives.

The Partnership Way is designed for use by all religious denominations, theological seminaries, and other groups and individuals that share the concern for helping us to move from a dominator to a partnership society. It is our hope that it can help us lay the spiritual foundations for a world where *hochma* and *sofia* (the ancient feminine appelations for wisdom) can truly rule and *agape* (or sisterly *and* brotherly love) can guide our interpersonal and international relations.

The Partnership Way
for Addiction and
Codependency
Recovery Groups

All over the United States, and now also in other parts of the world, women and men are coming together to help themselves and their loved ones recover from patterns of addiction and codependency. Only a short time ago addiction was associated with only alcohol or drugs. But today we are beginning to recognize, in the words of Anne Wilson Shaef, that ours is an addictive society: that patterns of addiction—be it to compulsive eating or to work, to mechanical sex or to abusive relationships—are more the norm than the exception. Along with this has also come the growing recognition that addiction and its correlate, codependency, stem from what psychologists call dysfunctional families: families in which children are routinely physically and/or emotionally abused.

How did all this come about? Why would so many people (seemingly the vast majority) get themselves into these miserable situations? It does not seem to make much sense, considering that avoiding pain and seeking pleasure are the most basic human (as well as animal) impulses. And why would they stay in such a painful fix?

Armies of psychiatrists, psychologists, and social workers have been trying to answer these questions by looking at people's personal and family histories. That is certainly an important first step.

But when millions of people are enmeshed in dysfunctional addictions and codependent relations, the problem is clearly not just personal, but social. We have to look not just at our personal and family histories, but at our social and cultural history. The basic question that we have to address is, what in a social system can make people literally go against their natural pain-avoidance and pleasure-seeking impulses?

THE PARTNERSHIP AND DOMINATOR ALTERNATIVES

The dysfunctional family—based on control and fear—is the kind of family that is required to maintain and perpetuate what we have called a dominator society: a way of organizing social relations held together by control through fear, denial, and ultimately force. Sometimes referred to as the traditional or patriarchal family, it rank orders human relations through dominator/dominated roles, beginning with the stereotypical dominator/dominated roles women and men are required to play. This was the kind of family that went along with traditions such as slavery, serfdom, and the "divine right of kings to rule."

It was in this dominator family that both boys and girls were conditioned to fit into a dominator society, learning to repress and deny their pain and anger, to deflect it against "inferior" or "dangerous" people, and to carry feelings of mistrust and betrayal into all social relations, thus keeping the whole system in place. And both mothers and fathers then passed these patterns of family relations on from generation to generation, thus unwittingly maintaining not only the dominator system, but also the pain and misery we are now beginning to recognize as stemming from dysfunctional homes.

The exciting thing is that today so many people are no longer accepting ways of thinking and living that not so long ago were viewed as "just the way things are." It is exciting not only for the immediate personal lives of those involved, but for society as a whole. For by challenging ways of relating based on denial and control, we are effectively challenging the very foundations of a dominator society. And by questioning old adages such as "spare the rod and spoil the child" and the inevitability of the "war of the sexes," we are beginning to leave behind the habits of behavior required to maintain a social system where "strong-man rule" (be it in the home or state) and the subordination of women (and all that is considered "feminine" or "weak" in men) is considered normal and necessary by both women and men.

The Partnership Way is designed to help take this process an important step further. It is designed to help women and men working in Twelve-Step and other recovery groups more effectively deconstruct not only the belief systems, but also the day-to-day practices, that have imprisoned us in unhealthy and painful ways of relating to ourselves and others. Most important, it is designed to help us move from deconstruction to reconstruction, to the creation for ourselves and our children of more satisfying and humane partnership alternatives.

Just as the dominator family is the training ground for living in a warlike, male-dominant, and basically authoritarian (or dominator) society, the partnership family is where we can learn to live in a more peaceful, just, and mutually satisfying way. Here neither women nor men have to be imprisoned in the rigid straightjackets of roles that deny them part of their humanity. Here the bringing up of children is not mainly through fear or negative conditioning but primarily through the positive conditioning that rewards helpful and responsible behaviors. And here both little girls and little boys have the opportunity to develop self-esteem, along with attitudes and behaviors that make it possible for them to live with others in the mutually respectful and cooperative way required for a pluralistic and truly democratic, or partnership, world.

SELF-HELP PROGRAMS

The basic premise of self-help programs, such as Twelve-Step programs, is that through partnership—through sharing of feelings and ideas, mutual respect, and, above all, mutual empowerment—we can heal ourselves. But the construction of a partnership society requires more than recovery, it requires renewal and growth.

The materials that follow offer a rich source of both new information and experiential work that can enrich and broaden Twelve-Step and other self-help programs. In addition, the nine sessions can be utilized to form parallel partnership groups. And for those who are ready to move beyond personal healing to the essential social healing, they offer tools for both personal and social transformation.

It is our hope that in helping us understand that our problems stem not from our personal shortcomings or perversities, or even from those of our mothers and fathers, but rather are rooted in an unhealthy and imbalanced dominator social system, *The Partnership Way* can help us more successfully deal with our negative feelings, particularly our feelings of guilt and shame. It is also our hope that *The Partnership Way* will be a catalyst for developing positive feelings, images, and actions that can more effectively guide our recovery, both emotionally and spiritually.

We recognize the enormous contribution of the Twelve-Step programs and believe it is essential that we learn to acknowledge and seek guidance from our higher selves, whether we call this God, Goddess, or higher spirituality. At the same time, we are also concerned about an element of disempowerment in the constant reiteration that we are powerless. It is certainly true that as addicts or codependents we are powerless to control our situations as long as society keeps driving us to addiction and codependency. But it is also true that working together we have the power to change ourselves and society—and that unless we do, we will indeed remain powerless.

For power in the best sense is not control and domination over others, but the power to create for ourselves and our loved ones better partnership ways of relating. *The Partnership Way* is designed to help us reclaim that power.

THE PARTNERSHIP
STUDY GUIDE

This Study Guide is meant to be a catalyst for a creative journey.

Nothing is written in stone!

Have fun with it!

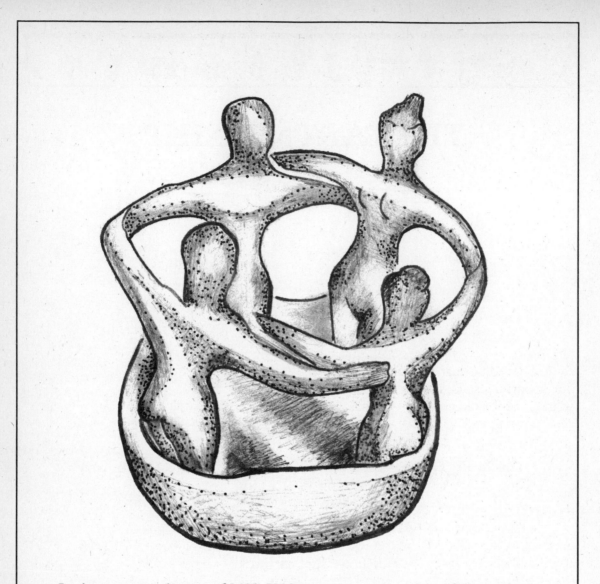

In these pottery dancers of 1400–1100 B.C., we see the origin of the modern Cretan dance "pentosalis." Made famous by the movie *Zorba the Greek*, dancers characteristically hold each other's shoulders. In early times this "partnership" dance was part of religious ceremonies. Line drawing from the original: Jim Beeman.

Introduction

This introduction is intended to help set the stage for the sessions that follow. Facilitators may want to integrate some of this material into their opening remarks at the first session.

Ours is a time of crisis, but also of opportunity. It is a time of great personal and social upheaval, a confusing and difficult time because we are realizing that many of the conventional ways of doing things are not good for us. But precisely because we are taking a fresh look at so many of the old givens—such as war, racism, sexism, wife battering, child beating, and rape—it is also a time of new hope and opportunity.

Many of us are reexamining ways of thinking and living that not so long ago were seen as "just the way things are." In the process, we are also beginning to see that we can create for ourselves more satisfying ways of living, that we *can* shift from a dominator to a partnership society.

In his book *Global Mind Change,* Willis Harman states: "Throughout history, the really fundamental changes in societies have come about not from dictates of governments and the results of battles but through vast numbers of people changing their minds—sometimes only a little bit." He points out that economic, political, and even military institutions persist because they have legitimacy, and that legitimacy comes from the perceptions of people. People give legitimacy and they can take it away. A challenge to legitimacy is probably the most powerful force for change to be found in history.

What we are now learning about the real possibility of constructing a partnership society powerfully challenges the assumptions that have given legitimacy to the dominator model. Even beyond that, by joining together to use this knowledge, we not only change our inner images of reality but we also begin to change every aspect of our world.

GOALS OF THE STUDY GUIDE

One goal of this study guide is to help us see the barriers to positive personal and social change, both inside and outside of us, that until now have been so taken for granted they have been invisible. By moving us beyond the probing of our personal and family histories to a new understanding of our social and cultural history, these sessions can help us see that our story as human beings is not as limiting and negative as we have been told. By exploring millennia-long traditions belonging to a time when the mainstream of our cultural evolution oriented primarily to a partnership rather than a dominator model, these sessions can also help us see that the chronic tensions, miseries, and bloodbaths of the last five thousand years have *not* been due to human nature but rather to a dominator detour.

A second goal of this study guide is to help us recognize patterns—that is, relationships between mutually reinforcing parts of a system. In the case of the dominator patterns, this helps us cut through the conventional confusion that has obscured our root problems. In the case of the partnership system, it helps us lay the foundations for new structures, new habits, that can better our lives and our world. Above all, it can help us see that how we relate to ourselves and to others on the personal level and the kind of society we live in—and even whether our global system can survive at this critical evolutionary crossroads—are inextricably interrelated.

A third goal is to help us build on these foundations, to construct for ourselves a new framework for positive personal and social action. Specifically, then, the most important purpose of this study guide is to help us *do* things differently. The purpose is not only to help us see that a more satisfying way of living and loving is possible, but also to experience that by working together in partnership we can integrate principles and habits of partnership into the deepest recesses of our hearts and minds. This can then provide the necessary foundations for a functioning partnership society.

PROCESS

But how do we learn to live, work, and love in partnership when so much of what we have been taught—from ideas like "a man should be the boss in his home" to stories and pictures idealizing "heroic conquest"—are thought and action scripts for domination rather than partnership?

The first step is to reexamine what has been presented to us as "traditional" stories and images, and at the same time learn about very different traditions that lasted for many thousands of years. This gives us a new contextual framework, offering us alternatives to what we have been taught is "just the way things are."

The second step is to use this new contextual framework to create *new stories and images* with which to write for ourselves new *thought and action scripts*. For it is through these new stories and images that we can give voice and shape to a powerful new vision of our present and future that can help us learn *new habits* of thinking, feeling, and acting.

We all can think of an example of change in our personal lives, whether it involved quitting smoking, or forming a new habit like eating less fat or sugar or regularly doing some kind of exercise. Even the most entrenched social attitudes can—and do—change, like the once-prevalent idea that slavery is only natural. Moreover, our most powerful social institutions can be altered, like the shift not so long ago from "divinely ordained" despotic monarchies to democratic republics.

But to make these changes, it is not enough that we analyze and discuss what we want to change. Learning involves not only reason but also emotion and action. To learn new and better ways of living, loving, and working, we have to involve *both* our linear, logical learning abilities and our emotions and intuitive faculties. Particularly, we need to improve our ability to see interconnections or patterns in a system as a whole if we are to take appropriate action for change. This is why these sessions are designed to integrate both intellectual and experiential learning as the basis for developing new modes of action.

The outline for each session includes a summary of its goals and a list of discussion topics. Equally important are the suggestions for getting started and closing, which are usually more experiential. These help to put us in direct touch with ourselves on a deeper level of our feeling and life experiences. By combining, on the one hand, focused study and stimulating discussion and, on the other, the imaging and experiencing of new patterns of thought, feeling, and action, we can more quickly learn to integrate ways of living, loving, and working in partnership into our day-to-day lives.

STRUCTURE OF THE STUDY GUIDE

The Partnership Study Guide is designed to serve a wide variety of users. For individual users or for facilitators with little experience, it can be used with a minimum of preparation. Or it can be a rich resource for more experienced facilitators who want to design their own study and discussion plan.

The *Nine-Session series* offers nine structured meetings. Each session consists of ten parts: Goals, Readings, Materials, Preparation for Facilitators, Getting Started, Further Exercises, Discussion Topics, Supplementary Readings, Preparation for the Next Session, and Closing.

Session 1 provides a process for the members of the group to get acquainted and together formulate commonly agreed-on goals and procedures. We recognize that in certain settings, such as university classes, it may be difficult or impossible to integrate this session into curriculum design, but we highly recommend its inclusion as it sets the tone for a partnership learning process.

Each session offers at least one experiential or participatory learning exercise and a number of discussion topics to choose from. Facilitators can easily plan a series by simply selecting the appropriate experiential exercise and/or discussion topics in each session. You will have to decide how much time you have and choose accordingly. You may want to use some of these suggestions in the order given; you may want to alter the order; or you may want to substitute some of your own goals, readings, exercises, and discussion topics.

The section Additional Exercises and Topics for Discussion provides materials for those who want to design their own longer or shorter series and/or supplement the basic materials in the nine sessions.

While the Partnership Study Guide offers a variety of options, it is basically geared to three levels of exploration:

- Individual growth and relationships
- Implications for our society and its institutions
- Our relationship to the natural world or cosmos

Not all the levels are addressed in every session, but the facilitators should keep them in mind during discussions and encourage the group to consider each level wherever appropriate.

It seems to be the nature of the partnership process that once you are under way with the right people, a natural flow tends to take over. Those who choose to be part of such a group are true explorers. Enjoy each other and the joint adventure that lies ahead!

The Nine Sessions

Women dancing. A fragment from 700 B.C. in Greece. Line drawing from the original: Jeff Helwig.

Session 1:
Getting Acquainted

GOALS

1. To get acquainted with one another.
2. To examine our goals for the series.
3. To begin to visualize better personal and social alternatives.

READINGS

None for this session.

MATERIALS

Large newsprint pads, easel, felt-tip pens, masking tape, name tags for group members, a sign-up sheet with room for group members to write names, addresses, and phone numbers.

Optional: A candle, a sturdy and safe candleholder, refreshments.

PREPARATION FOR FACILITATORS

- Prepare some introductory remarks or adapt the Introduction to the study guide for this purpose. Be prepared to introduce yourselves and to discuss the study plan with the group. Make a list of overall goals on newsprint, using the goals in the Introduction as guidelines and incorporating your own ideas.

- Familiarize yourselves with the outline of the nine-session program so you can tell the group briefly what it covers. (It is a good idea to write the session titles on newsprint.)
- Familiarize yourselves with the material under "Facilitating Experiential Learning" in the earlier chapter entitled "The Partnership Way for Group Facilitators and Teachers."
- Whenever possible, set up seating in a circle, as a circle helps to unify the group and makes conversation flow more readily.

GETTING STARTED

It is important to make sure members of the group get acquainted in a way that connects with the reason they have come and with their expectations.

A good way of doing this is for the facilitators to begin by introducing themselves, telling the participants why they brought this group together, and introducing the series. They can use their own introductory remarks or an adaption of (or excerpts from) the Introduction to the study guide. It is recommended that this segment take a maximum of ten to fifteen minutes.

The members of the group are then asked to briefly introduce themselves and tell the others why they are here and what they would like to take back with them. As the group members are sharing, it is important for the facilitators to record key words and phrases on large newsprint sheets. The phrases that are recorded will be used in the process of forming group goals and are also needed for the facilitators to write a summary of the first meeting.

SETTING GROUP GOALS

When members are sharing their goals, they should be encouraged to frame them in positive terms—in other words, in terms of what they want rather than what they don't want.

After everyone else has expressed their hopes and expectations, the facilitators can then share what they expect to get out of the sessions. This too is recorded on the newsprint. *It is very important for the facilitators to have thought this through and to be able to clearly communicate a positive image of the expected outcome—again, very specifically, what you want rather than what you don't want.*

This would also be an appropriate time for the facilitators to put up the goals for the series they have prepared before the session and to invite the participants to compare and notice the similarities and differences between the overall goals the facilitators have just put up and the individual goals that the participants have shared.

Then the participants are asked to decide which goals this particular group feels are most important in relation to their stated hopes and expectations. Again, it is important for things to be stated in positive terms and as specifically as possible. This is the first step in a participatory or partnership process and can be used as an example during future sessions.

A good way to close this introductory and goal-setting segment would be to remind members that the goals may change as the sessions go on. Also, this is an appropriate time to increase the participants' awareness of how the partnership process worked for them.

Suggest that they do not evaluate the process in terms of "good" or "bad" but simply take an observer position. Sometimes it helps to explain that taking this position is like watching a movie and just observing the action. Then the participants can take their observations away as food for thought and perhaps become aware of what in themselves or others either facilitates or impedes the partnership process.

In those situations where it is appropriate and time permits, you may want to take a short break now. Obviously, each group will be different and the amount of time it has taken to get to this point in the session will vary depending on the size of the group and the skills of the facilitators.

FURTHER EXERCISES

Those groups that have enough time left can try any or all of the suggested exercises that follow. You, as facilitators, will have to decide how to delete, combine, or integrate these suggestions.

If the group has taken a break, when it reconvenes the facilitators may want to suggest that this part of the meeting, as well as future sessions, open with a brief ceremony.

IDEAS FOR CEREMONIES

The idea of a ceremony or ritual may seem strange to some people at first. But in many ways we all use rituals in our daily lives: the handshake as a greeting ceremony; the exchange of cards; blowing out candles at birthday parties to celebrate our birth; or the clinking of glasses to toast the pleasure of being together.

Developing a ceremony to open meetings can serve as both a way of helping to form group bonds and taking the participants into a more relaxed and centered space. However, this ceremony should not be imposed and should be handled with sensitivity.

One of the facilitators could light a candle and explain that this is probably a very ancient opening ceremony, since the light and warmth of fire has linked members of a community since the dawn of human society. Or you might ask the group if they want to do a brief breathing exercise. One of the facilitators would then ask people to close their eyes, take three deep breaths, and observe their own breathing for a few minutes.

There are many possible variations, but the aim is to help people feel they are embarking on a special adventure together and to relax. We all are very busy and lead complex lives. It is important to help the members of the group leave behind their tensions and cares, at least for a while.

After the brief ceremony or breathing exercise, the following process is a good way to help people get in touch with each other and with their feelings.

VISUALIZING A PARTNERSHIP WORLD

When the participants are relaxed, ask them to close their eyes and visualize, as clearly as possible, what the world would be like if women and men were equal partners. Invite the group to be as specific as possible. What would they see, what would they hear, what would they feel? If they were writing, producing, and directing a movie of a world where men and women were equal partners, what would that movie be like?

The following questions may be of help:

- What do you think our lives would be like if there were equal partnership between women and men?
- How would it affect our self-image as women and men?
- How would it affect our family relations?
- Would international relations differ? Race relations?
- Would our religious institutions change?
- How would it affect our education?
- Would the corporate sector and the workplace be altered?
- How would it affect social priorities?
- Would there be changes in entertainment, art, and humor?
- What kinds of things would be considered funny?
- What would be most highly valued and rewarded?

When you can sense that people are finished, ask them to open their eyes and divide into dyads and take ten to fifteen minutes to share their "movies" with each other.

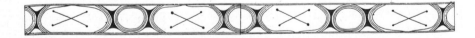

SHARING VISIONS

Each person takes a turn being the "storyteller" while the other is the listener. Some people will take to working in dyads easily, but for some it will be unfamiliar and they may start off by feeling uncomfortable. It may therefore be a good idea for the facilitators to deal with this openly, to invite group members to view it as a new adventure, something like traveling in a foreign country with different customs. It may feel alien at first, but therein lies the fun and richness of new discovery.

You may also want to suggest that individuals pair up with someone they don't know. Emphasize that the job of the listener is to listen and not to evaluate or judge the "story" of the other person.

This experience will help to establish that first important one-to-one link: the kind of closeness that is most easily felt with just one other person. It gives everyone a chance to be heard as well as to listen. Perhaps most important, it builds trust and a feeling of belonging. Individuals can begin to understand others' realities with their similarities and differences.

To stay on schedule and make sure there is enough time for the larger group discussion, the facilitators should set a time limit (perhaps ten to fifteen minutes) for the dyad work and also remind the dyads when it is time to begin to wind up. When the participants return to the larger group, the sharing continues.

This discussion will naturally lead to the question of what the major obstacles to equal partnership between women and men are. A good way to focus the discussion and also end on a positive note is to talk about areas where these obstacles are beginning to be addressed, such as family therapy and the current reexamination of dominator/dominated sexual stereotypes and the idealization of "man's conquest of nature." Also ask participants to think of areas that are not yet being addressed and focus on one such area.

DISCUSSION TOPICS

Since this first session is geared toward establishing group connections and introducing the participants to partnership group process, there may not be time for discussion questions. If there is time, you could introduce one of the discussion topics from Session 2 or choose one from the Additional Exercises and Topics for Discussion section.

SUPPLEMENTARY READINGS

None for this session.

PREPARATION FOR THE NEXT SESSION

Remind participants of the readings for the next session and ask them to bring their own copies of *The Chalice and the Blade* to each session. Ideally, participants should also have and bring their own copy of *The Partnership Way* for the additional readings and for their own Partnership Way Personal Journal. Otherwise, facilitators need to be responsible for a great deal of copying for handouts, beginning with the readings assigned for Session 2.

Facilitators should also plan to bring an example of a chalice and a blade to the next meeting and could suggest to participants that they can also do so if they want. (This can be anything from a kitchen cup and table knife to a collapsible camper's cup and hunting knife.)

CLOSING

In preparation for closing the meeting, you may want to ask the group if they want to close with a ceremony. Explain that people may need to relax after this intensive journey. Sharing a closing ceremony and formally opening the circle can help make the transition back to everyday life easier.

You may want to use blowing out the candle as a signal that the session has concluded. Some groups may want to repeat the breathing exercise or play a tape of relaxing music. Whatever feels comfortable to the participants is the way to go.

When and if the participants decide on a ceremony, set the stage for the next session and take care of any unfinished business before using the ceremony to close the session.

HELPING OUR MAILING LIST GROW

Please be sure to send a list of the names and addresses of participants to the Center for Partnership Studies, Box 51936, Pacific Grove, CA 93950, right after the first meeting so they can be added to our mailing list. If new members join the group, please update the list.

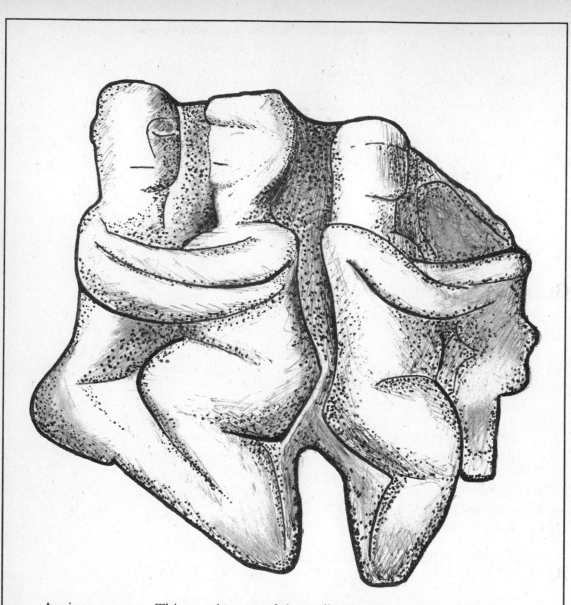

Ancient partners. This may be one of the earliest representations of the *hieros gamos*, or "sacred marriage." Linked together in the original carving in greenish-gray stone, to the left we see a couple embracing; to the right is the result of mother and child. This scene of ancient partners dates back to 6000 B.C. Line drawing from the original: Jim Beeman.

Session 2:
Crisis and Opportunity

GOALS

1. To begin to look at the kinds of relationships we experience every day and how the current crisis in sex roles is also an opportunity to rewrite our personal and social life scripts.
2. To begin to identify elements of partnership and dominator models in our own experiences.
3. To begin to explore how our personal and global problems relate to a dominator system and how a lot of our contemporary crises are also opportunities for accelerating the movement to partnership.
4. To explore the meaning of the chalice and the blade as symbols and their implications for our world and our lives today.

READINGS

- *The Chalice and the Blade:*
  Introduction
- *The Partnership Way:*
  All dominator and partnership model charts and explanatory materials in the Partnership Resources section in this guide ("The Partnership and Dominator Models: Basic Configurations," "The Partnership and Dominator Models: How to recognize them . . . ," and "Everyday Partnership Action Chart").

MATERIALS

Newsprint pads, felt-tip pens, masking tape, name tags for group members, an example of a chalice and a blade.

Optional: A candle and candleholder, refreshments.

PREPARATION FOR FACILITATORS

- Remember to bring your copies of *The Chalice and the Blade* and *The Partnership Way*.
- Put up the summary statements of the last meeting for people to refer to as they discuss their thinking and experiences since then.
- Write the title of this session on newsprint and be prepared to write summary statements of this session as well.
- Optional: If group members have agreed, make copies of the sign-up sheet passed around at the first session, to hand out to group members so they have one another's phone numbers and addresses.

GETTING STARTED

An alternative to opening with a ceremony would be for people to take turns reading a particularly meaningful passage from the readings for the session.

After the agreed-on opening, a good way to get right into the material for this meeting is to use the following free-association exercise.

FREE ASSOCIATION WITH THE CHALICE AND THE BLADE

Ask the participants to free-associate by saying whatever comes into their minds as they focus on first the chalice and then the blade that you or group members have brought, with one of the facilitators listing the associations on a sheet of newsprint.

Someone is sure to mention nurturing and feeding in response to the chalice. Someone else may talk about it as a spiritual symbol of actualization and transformation. Its association with the "feminine" and with the ancient Goddess as a source of life and nurturance may also come up.

The blade will probably be seen by some as a symbol of taking rather than giving life. Others may talk of it as expressive of a culture like that of some of the Indo-European barbarians that overran Europe (who, as UCLA archeologist Marija Gimbutas writes, literally worshiped the lethal power of the blade). Still others may relate the blade to the still-prevailing "conquest of nature" mentality, and in turn link that to our equation of "masculinity" with conquest—be it of women, other men, or nature.

Some of the discussion will undoubtedly focus on how the blade has become the symbol of a dominator view of power in a society where blades are mythologically associated with the "masculine." From this perspective the chalice represents a more "feminine" view of power: power from within oneself; power with, rather than over, others; enabling and supportive rather than dominating and destructive power.

But there will probably also be some discussion of an aspect of the blade that transcends and antedates the dominator system. This is the blade as an early tool for harvesting wild grains and tanning hides—a tool used by and associated with women *and* men. This can easily lead to the question of sexual stereotypes of "masculine" domination and action versus "feminine" subservience and passivity, and how these stereotypes are today being challenged.

Everyone can join in this discussion even if they have not given these things much thought before, and this way the meanings come directly from the group. Also, each person can be asked to free-associate the meanings of these symbols to specific experiences and patterns in his or her own life.

FURTHER EXERCISES

Either as a supplement or as an alternative to exploration of the chalice and blade symbology opening exercise, participants can

53

be asked to close their eyes and wait for images to come that they associate with first the chalice and then the blade.

They can be asked to pick up a chalice or imagine picking one up and holding it. Ask them, "How does it feel?" "What can you do with it?" Then they can do the same with the blade. The group can talk about these images and perhaps draw them on the newsprint. They can be asked to note the differences in the feelings and images they associate with each item.

The participants can then be asked to put these images in the context of the alternatives of the partnership and dominator models and how our definitions of what is "masculine" and "feminine" would be different in each of these models. They could also be asked to think of how, in a partnership society, masculinity would not have to be equated with conquest and domination and how in such a society qualities such as caring and compassion as well as assertiveness and self-expression could be considered appropriate and desirable for *both* men and women.

Participants could also be asked to think of all the images of weapons that are portrayed on television, and the frequency with which they are seen. Facilitators can make a list on newsprint. Then ask the group to come up with all the images of the chalice they can think of and the frequency with which they are portrayed. Make a list on a separate piece of newsprint. Give people a few minutes to notice the differences and then ask them to imagine what it would be like if the chalice imagery of enfolding and nurturing were seen more frequently and the blade images of cutting and destruction were reduced.

DISCUSSION TOPICS

Select one of the following three topics for discussion to begin with. Use another if time permits.

1. Many of us are exploring new ways of relating to one another. We are discovering that the old models of relationship do not really work, and are seeking better alternatives. A way of cutting through some of the confusion is to look at our exploration as an attempt to shift from dominator/dominated to partnership relations

(see charts on pp. 179–90 in the section Partnership Resources) and to ask ourselves to look at our own relationships from this new perspective.

The following questions can help stimulate this discussion:

- When have you been dominated? What did it feel like?
- How did you cooperate with this?
- What do you think you might do differently now?
- When have you been a dominator? What was that like for you?
- What were its advantages? Its disadvantages?
- When have you participated in a partnership? What was that like for you?
- What were its advantages? Its disadvantages?
- How do you think you received social support for a partnership relationship?
- How do you think it was opposed or undermined?

2. The Introduction to *The Chalice and the Blade* shows that we have been taught a limited vision of alternatives. For example, we tend to think that the opposite of patriarchy is matriarchy without realizing that they are both dominator models and that the real alternative is partnership.

   We have also been taught to divide the world into opposing camps such as religious vs. secular, capitalist vs. communist, developing world vs. developed world, light-skinned vs. darker-skinned races, and so on. To gain real insight into how these systems and structures affect humanity, it is useful to look at the dominator or partnership aspects in each of them.

   The following questions can help stimulate this discussion:

   - How does the distinction between patriarchy and matriarchy differ from that between the dominator and partnership models?
   - How does thinking in terms of partnership and domination cut through conventional polarities such as religious vs. secular or communism vs. capitalism?
   - Name or identify partnership and/or dominator aspects of particular religions, philosophies, and political

structures, focusing particularly on contemporary trends toward partnership and the dominator resistance.

Allow plenty of time to discuss these questions, not only in this session, but also in later ones, because our awareness deepens and broadens over time.

3. Many of our contemporary global crises—such as environmental pollution and the threat of nuclear holocaust—are the result of the emphasis a dominator system places on so-called masculine values of conquest and domination. For example, in the United States almost 60 percent of every tax dollar has gone to financing foreign intervention, nuclear weapons, and other military expenditures, with only a fraction of it left (after interest payments on the national debt) for human services. And in the poorest, most overpopulated, and most warlike and violently repressive "developing" regions of the globe such as parts of the Middle East and Latin America, women and so-called feminine values such as caring and nonviolence are most suppressed and despised.

The following questions address this topic as well as the growing awareness that a fundamental shift in priorities is essential.

- Why do you think that all over the world today there is so little social priority given to so-called women's issues?
- Do you think we would have massive overpopulation if women had free access to both birth control technologies and equal educational and job opportunities?
- Do you think the fathers who today see their role as including the traditional "feminine" mothering will be less likely to consider warfare "manly" and "fun"?
- Why do you think the modern feminist movement has met with so much resistance from both the extreme right and left?

4. Many of our contemporary crises are also opportunities to develop new and better ways of living, working, and loving. For example, on the personal level, the changing roles of

56

women (and men) are sometimes confusing. But they are also opening many new options to both women and men.

On the social level, we have seen the piecemeal replacement of old dominator forms (like the despotic rule of kings over their "subjects" and of men over the women and children in the "castles" of their homes) with more democratic families and states, where linking rather than ranking is the primary organizational principle. But such fundamental social changes cannot happen without a certain degree of social and personal dislocation.

- Why do you think some people focus on the "breakdown" of the family and others recognize that if new partnership family forms are to emerge, the older dominator family forms cannot remain in place?

- Why do you think that people are more likely to deny and suppress their real feelings in a dominator society?

- How do you think the modern development of psychology relates to the movement toward a partnership society?

- How do you think current psychological priorities support or impede the movement toward partnership?

- How do you think the civil rights movements and the struggle against racism and colonialism are central to the modern partnership thrust?

- How do you think rapid technological changes have worked in creating for us both crises and opportunities?

Where the group is large and has broken into smaller groups, it is especially important to have a general discussion of what emerged in the small groups and to tie it back to the Introduction to *The Chalice and the Blade,* especially the concept of the two models of society—dominator or partnership—based on ranking or linking.

Also be sure to write on the newsprint the major themes that emerge in this and subsequent sessions. This will provide a kind of group history, and these sheets can be put up at the beginning of each meeting to provide the group with a sense of continuity and identity.

Ask the members what was particularly helpful and interesting in this session and what they would like to repeat or do differently next time.

SUPPLEMENTARY READINGS

None for this session.

PREPARATION FOR THE NEXT SESSION

Remind participants of the readings for the next session and ask them to bring materials to share, such as books with good illustrations of Paleolithic and Neolithic art (see Supplementary Readings at end of Session 3), pictures and/or reproductions of Goddess figures, evocative music, or a tape of a relevant talk or discussion. Alexander Marshack's *The Roots of Civilization* would be a good source for pictures of "wrong-way weapons." (See also line drawing on p. 59 of *The Partnership Way.*)

CLOSING

As established during Session 1, or select from earlier suggestions.

This is a sketch of a carving of an antelope on a piece of bone dating back to 20,000 B.C. Next to the antelope are the "wrong-way arrows": for many years, authorities routinely identified these objects as arrows being shot at the antelope, even though these "arrows" curiously seem to be missing their mark. Through careful analysis Alexander Marshack proved these were not weapons, but *vegetation*—with the branches going the *right* way. Line drawing from the original: Jeff Helwig.

An early image of the Goddess found carved on a rock at Laussel, France, from Paleolithic times. This one is unusual in that she is holding what appears to be a horn of plenty in the shape of a crescent moon—a symbol later associated with Artemis or Diana, Huntress and Lady of the Beasts. Line drawing from the original: Jeff Helwig.

A goddess figurine found in Catal Huyuk, Turkey, dating back to 5750 B.C. She is seated on a throne, giving birth, while flanked by what are identfied by most authorities as two leopards. What is believed to be the tail of one of the leopards can be seen wrapped over her right shoulder. Line drawing from the original: John Mason.

Session 3:
Our Hidden Heritage

GOALS

1. To develop an awareness of the modern reappraisal of Neolithic agricultural societies and evidence that strongly suggests that in these societies
   - the world was imaged as a Great Mother who had both divine sons and divine daughters,
   - relations between women and men as well as between men and men, and women and women were generally equalitarian, and
   - war was virtually unknown.
2. To reexamine our personal and cultural values and assumptions in the light of this ancient alternative model.
3. To reexamine our feelings about the female and male bodies in light of this information.
4. To continue the reappraisal of our feelings about masculinity, femininity, and power in terms of the information presented in the readings for this session.

READINGS

- *The Chalice and the Blade:*
   Chapter 1, "Journey into a Lost World: The Beginnings of Civilization"
   Chapter 2, "Messages from the Past: The World of the Goddess"
   Maps and charts, pp. 243–48

MATERIALS

Regular supplies plus art books and pictures, particularly of Goddess images, and other materials brought by group members (see Session 2's section on preparation for this session).

PREPARATION FOR FACILITATORS

Same as for Session 2.

GETTING STARTED

Refer to last session's summary statements for some continuity and an opportunity for fresh insights. When appropriate, bring the group to this session's focus: our hidden heritage and its implications for our present and future.

The Paleolithic "Venuses" and the countless Neolithic Goddess figurines, statues, and other images are astonishing to most people. This is why it is important to have such pictures at this session. Begin by passing them around. Looking at these images where the sexual parts of a woman's body are often depicted as sacred is an effective way of accessing different ideas and feelings about our bodies and the consequences for our values and social organization.

After the participants have had a chance to look at these pictures, ask them to reflect on how we have been taught to view women's and men's bodies. In mixed groups, a good way to approach this question of our feelings about the female and male body is to ask the women and the men to form separate groups. This makes it easier for women and men to talk openly of their feelings and begin to reexamine how they have been taught to think of their own and women's bodies. It may also be effective to split the smaller groups into dyads.

FREE ASSOCIATION ON WOMEN'S AND MEN'S BODIES

In dyads, two women can share with each other what it felt like growing up and becoming aware of their changing bodies.

- What did it mean to them to "become women"?
- Was their first period presented to them as a "curse" or as welcome and natural?
- What were the body images presented to them as ideals?
- Were they taught to think of their bodies as a source of pleasure to themselves or to others—namely men?

Working in dyads may also make it easier for men to look more deeply into their feelings about women's bodies.

- Were they taught to see them as objects to be taken and used?
- How did the way they learned to look at their own bodies and their own sexuality relate to this?

This sharing of feelings about women's bodies and thus also images of women and femininity will inevitably bring out strong feelings. For some women, there will be painful feelings—feelings of inadequacy, of somehow failing to "measure up."

Discussion of these experiences usually goes easily into all the ways advertising tells us we are not OK but need to be thinner, smell better, have a different hair color, etc., and all the things various religious groups teach girls about covering or being ashamed of their bodies.

Men dealing with similar questions will also have strong feelings. For instance, the dominator model's rejection of the life-giving powers of the female body may translate into a rejection and alienation of all our bodies. This was the case in Western society, where the Church condemned all that is carnal, especially female bodies but also to some extent male bodies—all flesh.

It is also helpful for both men and women to examine how our images and feelings concerning the male body sharply differ from those about the female body. Thinking about the male body may yield an image of strength, action, and instrumentality, and a great deal less concern as to whether and how a particular male body differs from an arbitrary cultural ideal of what is "beautiful."

It may also be of interest to note how we generally pay great attention to and place great importance on the advantages of the male body, such as height and stronger bones and muscles, while the advantages of the female body, such as developed breasts, better-protected genitalia, the uterus with its creative capacity, and the lesser vulnerability to disease and to inherited weaknesses and disorders, tend to be overlooked or considered less important.

At some predetermined time, the women and men come together again into the larger group and share their feelings and thoughts. This discussion should easily lead into the whole issue of the "superiority" of men and the system of values that goes along with this.

FURTHER EXERCISES

VALUES AND GENDER

The following questions may be helpful in exploring the issue of values and gender.

- Why should so-called masculine values such as conquest, exploitation, or domination (be it of women, other men, or nature) have social priority?
- What lies behind the contempt expressed in much of our literary and folk tradition for women and so-called feminine values such as nonviolence and compassion?
- What really is a sissy (weak sister) or "effeminate" man?
- Is expressing empathy and caring really a weakness?
- How do you think the devaluing of women as a group with different physical attributes relates to the devaluing of other races as groups with different physical attributes?

In a society where the highest value is assigned to the power to give and sustain life incarnated in women's bodies,

- Would women suffer from "penis envy"?
- Would sex be "dirty"?
- Would killing people and destroying property in warfare be idealized?
- Would men be ashamed to be caring or "soft"?

RITES OF PASSAGE

A good way to end this portion of the session is to ask the participants to take a few minutes to imagine rites of passage for girls and boys that would assist their emergence into womanhood and manhood in a partnership society.

These questions may be helpful:

- What would these partnership rites of passage be like for boys and girls?
- In what ways could they be designed to celebrate and honor the unique differences of each gender?
- How would they differ from rites of seclusion during menstruation and after childbirth as a protection from "pollution" in tribes where women are dominated by men?
- How would you feel as a woman if you went through a rite of passage that was empowering and spiritually uplifting?
- How would you feel as a man going through such a rite?
- Try to imagine this for yourself and for your daughters and sons.
- How would you begin to design such rites and then work for their use and acceptance?

As in every session, the facilitators should use the newsprint pad to record the feelings and ideas shared by the members of the group.

DISCUSSION TOPICS

1. How does the way we have been taught to think of our bodies as women and men affect
   - Our self-image?
   - Our ideas about sex?
   - About religion?
   - About race relations?
   - About power?
   - About other major aspects of our lives?
   - Why do you think the pregnant female body, once so central, is so rare in dominator religious, artistic, and media images?
2. In Goddess-centered societies, what was likely to have been woman's self-image? Man's self-image?
   - How do you think these societies would react to some of our current images of "sex goddesses"?

67

- What are your reactions to the Paleolithic and Neolithic female images?
- Do you think the artists were women or men or both?

3. What view of humanness is reflected in the many androgynous images of the Goddess from the period of prehistory?

   - What are the implications of a reverence for the life-giving and sustaining powers of *both* the male and the female?

   - How might an androgynous view of divinity (ultimate reality seen as Mother *and* Father) affect the way we view ourselves? One another? The "feminine"? The "masculine"? Social and economic values and organizational structures?

4. How might relations between the sexes have differed in societies that regarded a Divine Mother as the source of all life and the progenitor of both divine daughters (Kore, Persephone) and divine sons (Horus, Attis)?

5. Discuss the persistent belief that civilization began with the warlike, hierarchic, and patriarchal empires of the Sumerians, the Assyrians, and the Egyptians, and that earlier social orders were "precivilizational" or even "savage."

   - What are the essential characteristics of civilization?
   - Were the agricultural societies of the Neolithic period civilized in the modern sense? Why or why not?
   - How do prevailing models of the necessary attributes of civilization reflect and reinforce the dominator system?
   - What are the implications of the modern rediscovery of an ancient alternative?

   This discussion may lead to the notion of "the selfish gene" and other biological and social theories on the "inevitability" of male dominance and war in the civilized order. Reading aloud excerpts from *The Nature of Human Aggression* or *Not in Our Genes* may prove useful (see the Supplementary Readings list that follows). These themes will continue to be important in later sessions.

6. How do shared cultural images of our deep past affect our view of the nature of human beings and human society? Of our present and future? Of masculinity and femininity?

- Consider the familiar cartoon pictures of club-wielding cavemen dragging women about by the hair. What role do these and other such misconceptions of our ancient heritage play in maintaining the dominator order?

SUPPLEMENTARY READINGS

For full titles and citations, see the References at the end of this book. This list is for those who want more to read on any aspect of this session.

Fritjof Capra, *The Turning Point*

Marilyn Ferguson, *The Aquarian Conspiracy*

Marija Gimbutas, *The Goddesses and Gods of Old Europe* and *The Language of the Goddess*

Mara Lynn Keller, "The Eleusinian Mysteries of Demeter and Persephone: Fertility, Sexuality, and Rebirth"

R. C. Lewontin, Steven Rose, and Leon J. Kamin, *Not in Our Genes*

David Loye and Riane Eisler, "Chaos and Transformation"

Alexander Marshack, *The Roots of Civilization*

James Mellaart, *Catal Huyuk*

Ashley Montagu, *The Nature of Human Aggression*

Vicki Noble, *Motherpeace*

Merlin Stone, *When God Was a Woman*

Ethel Tobach and Betty Rosof, eds., *Genes and Gender*

PREPARATION FOR THE NEXT SESSION

Ask the group to bring pictures of the architecture, frescoes, sculpture, and jewelry of Minoan Crete. Also, the cofacilitators and others may want to bring pictures of some of the nineteenth- and twentieth-century art that so remarkably recreates the Minoan imagery (for example, Toulouse-Lautrec, Matisse, Picasso, Brancusi, and of course the newer ecology art depicting dolphins and other marine life).

Particularly for younger groups or those comfortable with using a creativity exercise, the cofacilitators could in addition bring some modeling clay and/or other artistic materials. This would give the group a chance to experiment with the kinds of forms and images elicited in them by the art of Crete. People love to create, but our society generally relegates creativity to those judged to have "talent."

Remind participants of the readings for the next session. Ask them to look over the suggested Discussion Topics and be prepared to choose those of most interest. If someone does not have *The Partnership Way,* a group member should be asked to share or the facilitators should make and hand out copies of the discussion topics.

CLOSING

Before closing you might suggest that a celebration of some kind be planned for the next meeting. The celebration could include a potluck meal or the sharing of some special treat (fruits, baked goods, or whatever the group prefers). This sharing could be a symbol for a partnership ritual where both women and men share not only the eating together but also the planning *and* the preparation of the food. Often this is done at the last meeting of a series, and you may prefer to do it this way. However, also doing it at some halfway point is a good way of forming closer group bonds.

A goddess figurine from Minoan Crete. Done in the highly glazed ceramic technique known as faience, this goddess is one of two similarly bare-breasted "snake goddesses" dating back to the 1600 B.C. Holding snakes in both hands, she also has a cat sitting on top of her head. Felines were a symbol of the Goddess and her priestesses. Hence, after the dominator shift, in keeping with the drive to wholly discredit the earlier ways, we find the cat now associated with evil and the medieval "witch." Line drawing from the original: John Mason.

The famous bull dancers from a fresco at the Palace in Knossos, Crete. Particularly fascinating is the fact that the figure to the left holding the bull by the horns and the figure to the right tossing the acrobat are female—traditionally depicted as white in Cretan art. The central figure—traditionally red in color—is male. Line drawing from the original: Jeff Helwig.

Session 4:
The Essential Difference

GOALS

1. To discover something of the beauty and power of the civilization of Minoan Crete and how it presaged much that we value in ancient Greece and in our own time.
2. To reflect on "the essential difference" that animated the Minoan social order.
3. To begin to explore the ways in which the rediscovery of ancient patterns of possibility can add satisfying and creative new dimensions to our own lives and our own society.
4. To reexamine some of our archetypes of heroes and heroines and their implications for our lives and our planet.

READINGS

- *The Chalice and the Blade:*
  Chapter 3, "The Essential Difference: Crete"

MATERIALS

Regular supplies plus art brought by group members and optional artistic materials (see Session 3's section on preparation for this session).

PREPARATION FOR FACILITATORS

Same as for Session 2. For those groups that have decided to have a potluck this will be a shorter session and facilitators will have to pace it accordingly.

GETTING STARTED

Begin the meeting as before. By now the group will have worked out a comfortable and effective way of starting each session, which serves as a transition from the outside world to a regular time and place for relating and learning in partnership.

Ask participants to share what, in the readings and sessions, has been most important or meaningful and most distressing or difficult for them up until now. When appropriate, bring the group to this session's focus, "the essential difference" that was Crete.

To get into the material on Crete, one option is to start by looking at the pictures in the books the cofacilitators and other people have brought. Also, there are many line drawings of Minoan seals and other images in this book that people may want to talk about.

By looking at some of the pictures of Minoan art as well as contemporary art reviving these motifs, we can begin to explore the important question of what kinds of images reinforce partnership rather than dominator ways of thinking and living on this Earth. Even more specifically, we can begin to look at the archetypes we have been taught of women and men, and how we can create for ourselves new partnership heroes and heroines.

We have all been taught dominator ways of thinking and living. And although there are very strong pressures moving us in a partnership direction, much of our culture continues to reinforce the dominator ways.

A good exercise that highlights this and is also fun and creative focuses on the differences between dominator and partnership archetypes. It dramatically shows how heroes and heroines unconsciously give power to the particular roles that are required by either a dominator or partnership system.

In this exercise the participants are asked to work in dyads (in mixed groups, dyads of the same gender). The exercise begins with one of the participants role-playing one of the dominator heroines or heroes for a few minutes, or if that is difficult, at least telling a story about a heroine or hero, or talking about some examples or some of the characteristics that go with this particular archetype.

DOMINATOR HEROINES AND HEROES

If we look at many of our archetypal models for women, we see that they are appropriate for a dominator society. For example, women have to suffer greatly in such a system. This is why we find so many Suffering Heroines in our stories.

The Suffering Heroine can take a number of forms: She can be the Sacrificing Heroine, such as the selfless mother, daughter, sister, or wife (a very popular heroine in religious and classical stories). She can be the Masochistic Heroine, the woman who derives pleasure from her suffering (a very popular heroine in much of contemporary pornography).

Other heroines model passivity and incompetence. There is the Helpless Heroine, all the way from Sleeping Beauty to the classic cartoon of the woman tied to the railroad tracks, waiting to be rescued by a male hero. Then there is the Foolish Heroine (exemplified by the "dumb blonde"). Also popular are the Deranged Heroine or Romantic Madwoman (such as Ophelia in *Hamlet*), and the Fallen Woman (who is punished for being "dishonored" by a man), as well as the Dying Heroine (such as in *Love Story*), who often even has to pay with her life for freely choosing whom to love (as in the famous operas *Carmen* and *La Traviata*).

And we are all familiar with the Saintly Heroine (the holy virgin) and the Evil Heroine (going back to Pandora and Eve). These archetypes give power to the idea that unless they are superhuman (above all carnal or worldly desires), women are subhuman and thus must be controlled by men—for their own and everyone else's good. Another variation is the Scheming Heroine who is punished for asserting herself and/or seeking self-expression (such as Alexis in "Dynasty" and the stereotype of the unhappy, unfulfilled career woman).

Dominator heroines have their counterparts in dominator heroes. Along with the sacrificing mother, daughter, sister, or wife, we find the Outstanding Hero (the legendary winner, leader, strong man, or man at the top). Related to him is the Courageous Hero (almost always also a Violent Hero) for whom the Helpless Heroine is the standard foil and/or prize. The Omniscient Hero (the "divinely ordained" king or modern "expert") is a dominator complement to the Foolish Heroine.

The Hero as Warrior is almost always egged on to battle by some version of a passive dominator heroine. And perhaps the most pervasive image associated with masculinity is the archetype of the Lord, the Lord who rules from heaven, as the head of a government, or as the head of a household or lord of the castle that is his home.

Typical of Minoan Crete is this premilitaristic, premacho portrayal of the "natural" male. Rather than being forced to armor himself to do battle in the world, he can concentrate on something that makes more sense—being a fisherman and food provider. From a fresco in Minoan Thera, about 1500 B.C. Line drawing from the original: Jim Beeman.

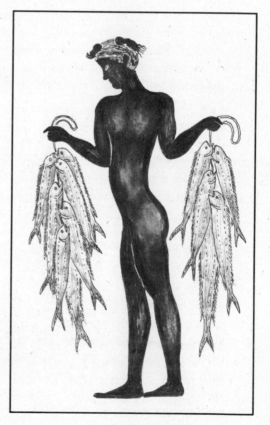

After about five minutes, the facilitator signals that it is now time to switch to the other member of the dyad to create a partnership alternative by either telling a story, role playing, or describing an alternative to the particular dominator archetype described by her or his partner.

PARTNERSHIP HEROINES AND HEROES

The partnership alternative to the Helpless Heroine is the Adventurous Heroine. In Minoan mythology, she could be a bull-dancer (as in the bull-leaping fresco) or the captain of a ship (as in one of the Minoan seals). Or she could be somebody like the astronaut Sally Ride in real life, the goddess Artemis in Greek mythology, or some of the newer science fiction heroines (from writers like Ursula LeGuin, or even the Sigourney Weaver role in films like *Alien*; however, without their simply stepping into the violent/courageous male role). Or in the sciences, she could be a primatologist like Jane Goodall or Diane Fossey (also played by Weaver in *Gorillas in the Mist*).

The alternative to the Foolish Heroine is the Wise Heroine. One example is the Crone, the ancient Wise Woman archetype now being reclaimed by feminist writers such as Mary Daly. More contemporary examples are the Woman as Counselor, such as the many women who are now in family and psychological counseling fields, and the Wise Mother as an antidote for "Father Knows Best." In science, she could be the Nobel prize-winning biologist Barbara McClintock, who pioneered an empathic, rather than purely objective, research method or psychiatrist Jean Baker Miller, whose work validates the wisdom of "feminine" caring and emphasis on the importance of relationship.

Instead of the Suffering Heroine we can have the Actualizing Heroine. By actualizing both herself and others, this woman shows that you do not have to actualize yourself at the expense of others. Contemporary examples are women artists and actresses who are also political activists such as Judy Chicago and Jane Fonda. Another alternative to the Suffering and/or Dying Heroine is the Happy Heroine who independently and freely chooses how to live and love, following both her heart and her mind.

77

A good alternative to both the Saintly and the Evil Heroine is the Spiritual Heroine. She can be a priestess of the Goddess such as Ariadne was in Crete. Or she can be a contemporary woman like so many of us today seeking to reclaim our birthright of direct connection to our higher and more spiritually enlightened selves.

An alternative to the Hero as Conqueror is the Hero as Healer. This can be a healer of the body who works in partnership with the person to be healed and does not just "give orders" as we have been taught to see doctors. It can be a man working to heal the Earth as an environmental or peace activist. Or it can be a man organizing groups such as Men Against Rape and other avenues for diagnosing and healing the male's identification with violence in a dominator society. Well-known models of social and spiritual healers in our time are Mahatma Gandhi and Martin Luther King, Jr.

An alternative to the archetype of the Hero as Warrior is the Hero as Mediator. As Mark Gerzon writes in *A Choice of Heroes,* "The Mediator does not require that life be a battle, nor does he equate heroism with fighting valorously; rather, the Mediator's heroic calling is to stand between the opposing armies. His goal is to enable the adversaries to coexist, if possible, to cooperate. He is not necessarily a pacifist . . . he is simply no longer enamoured with violence."

The partnership alternative to many of the stereotypical male heroes is the Hero as Nurturer. He can be a tiller of the soil or a fisherman (as in the Minoan fresco from the island of Santorini). He can be a teacher (however, one who does not feign omniscience). He can be a religious leader (but not one who pretends that he has a direct line to God or that because he is a man he is more spiritual than a woman).

In everyday life the Nurturer is the new father who is today emerging, freeing himself of the stereotypes of head of family/provider/king of his castle to explore and express his soft or "feminine" side. As Gerzon writes, "The Nurturer does not conceive children with the belief that someone else must take care of them. He sees himself as responsible for their growth as for their birth. . . . The Nurturer does not view spending time with his children as doing them or his wife a favor. He considers it a basic part of his life."

Another important alternative to the Macho Man or Hero as Warrior is the Sensitive Hero. This is the man who no longer feels that he has to suppress his feelings of empathy. It is also the "effeminate" or "effete" artistic man (such as the young man walking in a garden in the Minoan fresco, the "starving artist" characteristic of dominator history, or the many young men who are in our time learning that "real" men can—and do—have feelings other than disgust and anger).

Basically, what this exercise helps us do is to imbue with significance or "heroism" roles appropriate to a partnership-oriented culture, one where as in Minoan Crete the most valued role for *both* women and men is that of the Nurturer, once symbolized by the Great Goddess as the source of "the beauty, the passion, and the truth of love."

FURTHER EXERCISES

The following exercise can be used in addition to or instead of the preceding one.

JOURNEY TO CRETE

The cofacilitators ask the group to close their eyes, relax, and take a mental journey to Crete.

Imagine yourself as a woman or man living in Minoan times.

- What kinds of relationships do you form?
- What are your attitudes about sex?
- How are children taken care of and educated?
- How do you think of yourself in relation to nature?
- How do you experience spirituality?

After participants have created a "movie" based on these questions, the facilitators may want them to break into dyads or small groups and share the stories with each other. Then, the group could come back together and share their stories, noting the similarities and differences in the stories and the similarities and differences between their imagined story and their current reality. Encourage people to have fun and be as creative and outrageous as they can. After all, in a fantasy, magical things can happen.

As in every session, the facilitators should use the newsprint pad to record the feelings and ideas shared by the members of the group.

Those groups that feel comfortable with this may also want to tap their own creativity, either at this session or outside, by experimenting with the forms and images elicited in them by the art of Crete.

DISCUSSION TOPICS

1. What major characteristics distinguished Minoan Crete from other ancient civilizations with which we may be more familiar? What constituted "the essential difference"?

2. Does the changing face of modern life in America, Europe, or elsewhere reflect something genuinely akin to the "Cretan" spirit revealed in the archeological record? If so, what do such changes portend? If not, are apparent parallels only superficial? Consider such areas as

    • art, architecture, literature;

    • the social roles of the sexes;

    • religion, spirituality;

    • the "New Age," ecology, peace, women's, and other movements;

    • some of the new labyrinthine shopping malls;

    • women in sports; and

    • androgynous fashions for women and men.

3. What is the role of myth, archetypes, and symbols in establishing and maintaining a cultural paradigm?

    • Can you find similarities between the iconography and symbols of this earlier partnership-oriented culture and those emerging in movements focusing on peace, ecology, feminism, etc.?

    • Are we living in an age of "mythlessness" (that is, have the central stories and symbols of our culture begun to lose their meaning)?

4. What view of sexuality is reflected in the archeological record of Minoan Crete?

    • How does this relate to the modern "sexual revolution" and women's movement?

    • What are the social implications of a culture's outlook on sexuality? (The pictures of Minoan women and men are of slim people, with no huge differences in the musculature and size of women and men. We also learn from the bull-dancing fresco and other images that both women and men were athletic. This could lead to an interesting discussion of whether there is a relationship between the current revival of athletics for women and the trend toward a more relaxed and mutually satisfying sex life for both women and men.)

- What in the culture do you think contributed to the Minoans' evident joy in life?
- How do you think they resolved conflict?
- Why do you think they had no fortifications?
- Why do you think "feminine" sensitivity was expressed so vividly in their art?

5. Which sentence or paragraph in the assigned reading is most significant to you? Why?
   - In terms of your own life?
   - With respect to modern culture?
   - In its implications for the human condition?

SUPPLEMENTARY READING

For full titles and citations, see the References at the end of this book.

Harry Brod, *The Making of Masculinities*
Mary Daly, *Gyn/Ecology*
Mark Gerzon, *A Choice of Heroes*
Jacquetta Hawkes, *The Dawn of the Gods*
Nikolas Platon, *Crete*
Adrienne Rich, *Of Woman Born*
Karen Signell, *Wisdom of the Heart: Working with Women's Dreams*
Demaris S. Wehr, *Jung and Feminism: Liberating Archetypes*

PREPARATION FOR THE NEXT SESSION

Remind participants of the readings for the next session and, if someone does not have *The Partnership Way,* hand out copies of "The

Language of Partnership." Ask people to bring some materials to share that they feel symbolize the shift in our prehistory from a partnership to a dominator model as the main guide in our cultural evolution. This could be art or illustrations in books idealizing destruction and domination, such as scenes of heroic warriors, hallowed conquerors dragging prisoners in chains, or gods like Zeus raping women. Cofacilitators should also be sure to bring some materials themselves, including images of the Goddess as androgynous (like the one on the cover of *The Chalice and the Blade*). Images reflecting female-male complementarity, such as the Minoan Goddess figurines and male horns of consecration (showing the importance of the Bull or Horned God) are also useful and can be found in Platon's *Crete*. These serve as contrast to later images.

CLOSING

As appropriate.

Warriors from an ancient Roman mosaic. These figures vividly show the contrast between the earlier, more partnership-oriented art, and the emphasis on conflict, death, and pain that follow with the imposition of the dominator model. In the original, the figure shown vertical here is horizontal, having fallen, the other about to kill him. (If you turn the page, you can see this.) We have turned the figures this way because of the strange "dance of death" effect. Line drawing from the original: John Mason.

The murder of Penthesilea by Achilles, from an Athenian amphora, or vase, prior to the fifth century B.C. One of hundreds of thousands of precursors of our movie and TV killings, this was done in the big medium of that time, pottery, in the Black Figure technique, where for greater impact the black figure is silhouetted against the red ground of the pot. Line drawing from the original: John Mason.

Session 5:
The Interruption of
Civilization

GOALS

1. To reexamine the common assumption that prehistoric
   societies were primitive, matriarchal, and uncivilized, and
   that warfare, male dominance, and slavery are necessary
   characteristics of civilization; and to reflect on the degree to
   which these assumptions continue to influence our lives
   today.

2. To inquire more deeply into prevailing models of power,
   spirituality, and nature, and their personal and social
   consequences.

3. To begin to explore how the suggestion that a major
   cultural shift, a radical transformation in world view or
   paradigm that occurred in the ancient world, relates to the
   possibility that another such transformation may be under
   way today.

READINGS

- *The Chalice and the Blade:*
    Chapter 4, "Dark Order Out of Chaos: From the Chalice
    to the Blade," and Figures 6, 7, 8, and 9
    Chapter 5, "Memories of a Lost Age: The Legacy of the
    Goddess"

85

- *The Partnership Way:*
  "The Language of Partnership" in Partnership Resources.

MATERIALS

Regular supplies plus art brought by group members and cofacilitators (see Session 4's section on preparation for this session).

PREPARATION FOR FACILITATORS

Same as for Session 2.

Optional: The Victorian fantasy *Flatland* by Edwin Abbott also provides an excellent approach to the discussion of paradigm shift as the transformation of a culture's fundamental values and assumptions. A useful excerpt from this work can be found in Marilyn Ferguson's *The Aquarian Conspiracy,* pp. 65–66. Facilitators may want to bring copies for handouts.

GETTING STARTED

Begin the meeting as usual. You may want to begin by reading the following note from Riane Eisler:

"When I wrote *The Chalice and the Blade,* I was acutely, often very painfully, aware of how our Goddess heritage has been denied us in conventional religious and secular accounts, and how very difficult it therefore is for us to imagine a female deity. This is why Chapter 5 is subtitled 'The Legacy of the Goddess' and focuses on the Goddess and on women. But I think it is important to remember that there are also ancient male symbols of divinity, such as the many bucrania (bull horns) in Catal Huyuk shrines and the horns of consecration in Knossos and other Minoan sites.

As noted in *The Chalice and the Blade,* the bull seems to have represented the male life force. And the emphasis on the horned and hoofed animals in 20,000-year-old European caves could indicate that this symbology goes back all the way to the Paleolithic, where we often find paintings of animal pairs, female and male. In other words, just as the 'Venus' figurines prefigure the Great Goddess as the giver and nurturer of life, the Bull God (later discredited as the Devil) may also have very ancient roots.

I am adding these lines to again emphasize something that is, of course, an underlying theme in *The Chalice and the Blade* and my other works. This is that while the power to give and sustain life was conceptualized in female form (after all, life emerges from the female body), the male was also honored (and revered).

In short, while the Great Goddess was revered as the Mother of all Nature and Life, these were gender-balanced or partnership-oriented societies. Men, as well as women, played important roles. The critical difference is that, in contrast to dominator-oriented societies, here the male role and 'masculinity' were *not* equated with domination and conquest, be it of women, other men, or nature."

When appropriate, bring the group to this session's focus, the interruption of civilization. The facilitators can use the following exercise to lead this off.

LIVING IN A GREAT GODDESS WORLD

Ask the group to divide into dyads and then close their eyes, relax, and begin to imagine that they are living in a world that worships a Great Goddess, the Mother of all Nature and Life. (The pictures suggested in Preparation for this session could also be helpful here.)

Facilitators can use the following questions like a guided imagery (with some modification), or the questions can be put on newsprint and the group can read them together prior to doing the exercise.

- What does thinking of the Earth as our Mother feel like?
- What kinds of attitudes toward nature come with a belief system centering on a female deity representing creativity and the life-giving and regenerating powers of the universe? (Would "man's conquest of nature" be acceptable in such a society? How about man's conquest and domination of women?)

- What do you think your parents' relationship would have been like in this society where the Great Goddess had both divine sons and daughters?
- How would it have been different from the way it actually was? How would it have been the same?
- How would it have affected the way they felt and acted toward their children? Toward you as their daughter or as their son?
- How would it have affected their attitudes about war? About power? About women's and men's work? About what is moral and immoral? About different races and religions?
- How would it be reflected in language?

FURTHER EXERCISES

After the opening exercise has been processed, you can use the following additional exercise.

CHILDHOOD IN A GREAT GODDESS WORLD

Ask participants to imagine themselves as children in a society where a Great Goddess is worshiped—where in their homes, schools, and places of worship they learn many stories about this divine Mother and her divine daughters and sons.

Or ask them to imagine themselves as children in their own communities today sitting in a church, synagogue, or mosque worshiping a divine Mother and Father whose presence is manifested in all aspects of life and nature, whose love is our birthright as women and men. Also imagine that services are lead by both priestesses and priests.

Pose these questions:

- What is this like for you? How does it make you feel?
- How does it affect your attitudes about yourself? About women? About men? About nature? About power?
- How does it affect our language?
- How does it affect our views about what is normal and proper or ridiculous and unacceptable?

DISCUSSION TOPICS

1. Discuss how you think your family life has been affected by growing up in a world where men and "masculinity" were valued over women and "femininity"—as in the contempt men often feel for "women's work."

   - How do you think your generation is different from that of your parents?
   - What changes do you see in the next generation?

   Wherever possible, the discussion should be placed in the larger context of a major contemporary cultural shift—this time from domination to partnership as the guiding social image.

2. Discuss why the subordination of women and the feminine is so important in a dominator system.

   - How do you think sayings such as "If rape is inevitable, relax and enjoy it" or "All's fair in love and war" developed?
   - How do you think the subordination of women relates to racism and other ways of ranking one kind of human being over another based on inborn differences?
   - How do you think war and the "war of the sexes" are related?
   - Is world peace possible as long as the so-called hard or masculine values of conquest and domination are idealized?

3. How are our views about power, spirituality, and nature colored by the images, alternatively, of a male ruler of the universe like Jehovah or Zeus (who sits on a throne high above us and wields a thunderbolt or sword) or a Goddess whose body is a Universal Womb and whose symbols are trees, animals, and other aspects of nature?

   - To what degree do you or don't you have difficulty with the idea of a female deity? Why?
   - How does *The Chalice and the Blade* throw a different light on the story of the Garden of Eden and the legend of Atlantis?
   - Why do you suppose the gifts of civilization—the most fundamental of our technological and social

inventions—arose from earlier Goddess/partnership cultures?

- What would this kind of system have to do with basic creativity—for example, the invention of language, government, art, and law?

4. How would you describe the role of warfare in instituting and preserving domination and how does it relate to the definition of power as power over rather than power to or with? (You might find Jean Baker Miller's *Toward a New Psychology of Women* particularly helpful in defining different types of power. If groups engage in power exercises or simply list their understandings of what power is, they will come up with a mix of "power-over" and "power-for" ideas. Then the discussion can point out the difference. Again, the ideas come first from the experience of the participants. What is important is to see the implications of different definitions of power by looking at ancient society and then at our own.)

5. Discuss how language reflects and reinforces a dominator or partnership world view, and what changes in our language might dramatically alter the way we view the world.

SUPPLEMENTARY READINGS

For full titles and citations, see the References at the end of this book.

Edwin Abbott, *Flatland*

Roy Chamberlin and Herman Feldman, eds., *The Dartmouth Bible*

Marija Gimbutas, *The Early Civilization of Europe*

J. V. Luce, *The End of Atlantis*

Casey Miller and Kate Swift, eds., *Words and Women*

Erich Neumann, *The Great Mother*

Elisabeth Sahtouris, *Gaia: The Human Journey from Chaos to Cosmos*

Merlin Stone, *When God Was a Woman*

Nancy Tanner, *On Becoming Human*

PREPARATION FOR THE NEXT SESSION

Remind the members of the group of the readings for the next session. Ask them to bring one or two examples of what they feel could be typical dominator and, by contrast, partnership art.

CLOSING

As appropriate.

The goddess Athena. What has happened to the Goddess during the hybridization of the dominator shift is indicated by the serpent and vegetation of her old alliance on one side, and on the other, the spear and shield of the new regime. This figure was carved into a tiny personal seal in carnelian, found in Cyprus, dating to the fifth century B.C. Line drawing from the original: John Mason.

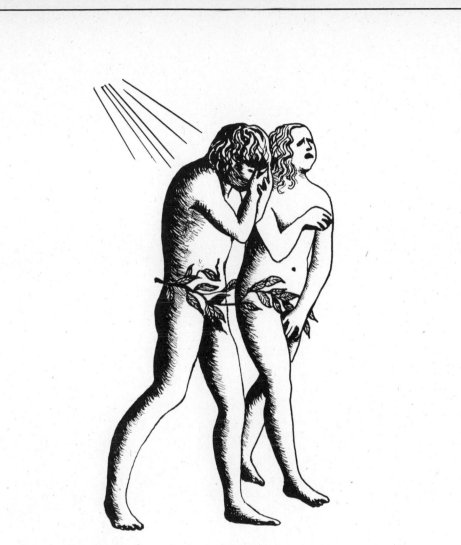

Adam and Eve being expelled from the Garden of Eden, from the fresco *Expulsion of Adam and Eve from Paradise* (ca. 1425) by the brilliant Renaissance painter Masaccio (1401–1428). Eve in this engraving, ashamed of her body and clearly with low self-esteem, contrasts poignantly with the self-assured, bare-breasted women of Minoan Crete. Line drawing from the original: John Mason.

Session 6:
The Great Cover-Up

GOALS

1. To begin to reassess conventional assumptions about morality, knowledge, and truth in light of the information examined in the preceding readings and sessions.
2. To relate this information to our own life experiences, particularly with respect to issues of control.
3. To reexamine our assumptions about reality, particularly in relation to the almost exclusive conventional focus in our schools and universities on the experiences and ideas of men.

READINGS

- *The Chalice and the Blade:*
    Chapter 6, "Reality Stood on its Head: Part I"
    Chapter 7, "Reality Stood on its Head: Part II"

MATERIALS

Regular supplies plus art brought by group members (see Session 5's section on preparation for this session).

PREPARATION FOR FACILITATORS

Same as for Session 2.

GETTING STARTED

The facilitators could begin by reading or telling an ancient story reflecting the remything process that so profoundly altered our perception of reality during the shift to a warlike, male-dominant, authoritarian society. For example, there are many myths of the old goddesses or their sons battling the new warrior gods, and having power forcibly taken from them. But there are also myths of the old goddesses marrying the new gods or being persuaded or tricked to hand over their power.

These myths are pertinent today. Women do not always battle openly because the conflict is often covert. Or if they do assert power openly, they often find themselves in trouble. On the other hand, men (who are in male-dominant societies supposed to have a monopoly on power), are also tricked into believing they can always be in control. In fact, much of their lives is directly controlled by other men who are their "superiors," and they are also many times manipulated by "inferiors" such as women.

Getting groups to engage in discussions of how women and men have personal power taken from them or allow themselves to be tricked into giving it away might be a way to begin examining more closely the interplay of partnership and dominator models in our personal lives.

The whole issue of control (of self and others) versus trust also directly leads back to the basic question of how we define power: as power over or power to and with. It further leads to the whole question of myths about the roles of women and men and the realization that attempts to maintain superiority or dominance are inimical to any really satisfying or partnership relationship.

FURTHER EXERCISES

Those groups that wish to do more experiential work may decide to use the following provocative guided visualization, which is adapted in part from a role-reversal exercise developed by Theodora Wells.

THE FLIP-FLOP WORLD

Ask the participants to relax in the usual way. Then explain that this guided visualization is intended not only to help us experience a gender role reversal, but also to gain insight into what it might have been like to have one's whole world view literally stood on its head through new and very different stories and myths about what is human nature and/or divinely ordained.

It is very important to stress that the purpose of this visualization is to help us feel how profoundly myths shape our view of ourselves and of what we consider reality. On one level, this exercise is a way of raising awareness about the arbitrary nature of some of our most hallowed assumptions. On another, and even more important level, it makes it possible for us to see that matriarchy is indeed the other side of the coin of the dominator model, and that a very different type of mythology has to be constructed to support a partnership society.

Ask the participants to close their eyes and go back to their childhoods and imagine that they have been born into and have grown up in a world where the following realities exist.

- Practically every time one picks up the newspaper or turns on the TV to find out what the world's leaders are doing, the pictures and names are those of women.
- When top religious leaders speak or write, they are usually women talking or writing about what women popes, bishops, and spiritual leaders have done or are doing.
- The prevailing view of the nature of women and men stresses that there are obvious biological explanations for women's leadership. Women are the life-givers, and their bodies are the incarnation of life-giving and life-sustaining power. Moreover, female genitals are compact and internal, protected by the body, while male genitals are external and exposed. Hence women are naturally meant to be the protectors of men, whose activities must be controlled for their own good and the good of the race, lest their reproductive vulnerability threaten the continuity of the human race.
- It is widely believed that in sexual intercourse the male genitals are engulfed by the protective body of the woman.

Males yearn for this protection, fully realizing their masculinity at this time—or a man only experiences himself as a "whole man" when thus engulfed. If a male denies these feelings, he is unconsciously denying his masculinity.

- Women are not only protective and controlling of men; they also must exclude them from dangerous and unsuitable activities. Sometimes this may seem cruel, as when a boy's sisters jeer at him when he runs or climbs because his primitive genitals flap around foolishly. But while girls can develop their bodies and minds freely in preparation for the active responsibilities of womanhood, males must be taught to be less active. Moreover, sheltering men in the homemaking virtues is both moral and natural, as in this way the males' passive nurturing role in the family balances the biological contribution of the woman to the race through pregnancy and childbirth.

- The superiority of women is also reflected in the language, where *woman* and *womankind* are generic terms that quite literally include *man* in them. Books, movies, plays, and courses of all kinds are thus called "The Story of Woman" or "The Study of Woman"—as everyone knows this also includes men.

Ask the participants to imagine that it has always been this way, every day of our lives. Ask them to feel what it would be like being born into such a world, growing up in it (either as girls or boys), becoming adults, experiencing what it means to be a woman or a man.

Ask them also to imagine what would happen once men found out this had not always been so—and all the pressure there would be to suppress this information.

Finally, ask them to imagine what could be done to make this a more balanced partnership world: particularly what kinds of stories and images could help such a change, how morality, good, and evil could be redefined, how women's and men's roles could be redefined in a way conducive to equal partnership rather than one-sided control and domination.

Then ask the group to share these ideas, feelings, and blueprints for a more balanced partnership future and, as always, note these on the newsprint pad.

DISCUSSION TOPICS

1. Discuss more recent attempts to rewrite history and compare them to the remything that took place in our prehistory.

   - Do the Stalin era, the McCarthy hearings, or more recently, the activities and pronouncements of groups like the Moral Majority reveal similar dynamics? What about Khomeini's "Islamic Revolution" in Iran and the teaching that women are dangerous and must be controlled for their own good and the good of the society?

   - What kinds of myths have been most significant in imposing and maintaining male dominance and authoritarianism?

   - What message about human nature is imparted by the Adam and Eve and Cain and Abel stories? About the "inevitability" of war and the war of the sexes? About "man's innate violence"? About how men, and especially women, have to be controlled "for their own good"?

   - After reading Chapter 7, what are your thoughts about the relation between politics, economics, and codes of morality? What are your feelings about the story of Lot and other biblical accounts where "moral" men directly or indirectly abuse and even murder women and children?

   - Many religions seem to believe and teach that human suffering and injustice are inevitable, even holy. How do you think this belief system perpetuates a dominator society? What kind of belief system do you think a partnership society would have to explain human suffering and injustice? How would it be different?

2. What new insights can we bring to bear on the study of religious and secular classics that idealize the dominator system (for example, passages in Greek literature, in the Bible, or even in the works of Shakespeare that idealize armed conquest and male dominance)?

   - Should the classroom presentation and discussion of such materials be changed? If so, how?

- What are the implications of the challenge to the dominator model for the established religious traditions? Is a transformation of existing religious patterns and structures likely or possible?

3. How can the information now being gathered by feminist scholars and others about the past and present of the ignored female half of humanity be integrated into our schools and universities?

4. Some people think that the advent and elaboration of the patriarchal and dominator motifs came about because of a deliberate cover-up of the ancient order and an effort to hide the truth. Some people think that it was not so much a matter of a deliberate attempt to hide the truth, but rather the ancient order was suppressed by those who failed to recognize its value. What do you think?

5. What are the consequences of identifying children exclusively by the surname of the father? Sharon Lebell's book *Naming Ourselves, Naming Our Children* deals with this issue. It raises questions like the following:

   - Should children bear their mother's and father's names—and in which order?
   - Should they select their own names?
   - How practical are alternatives to present custom?

6. What other feelings, thoughts, and memories have been evoked by reading these chapters and discussing the questions?

SUPPLEMENTARY READINGS

For full titles and citations, see the References at the end of this book.

Roy Chamberlin and Herman Feldman, eds., *The Dartmouth Bible*

Carol Christ and Judith Plaskow, eds., *Womanspirit Rising*

Scott Coltrane, "Father-Child Relations and the Status of Women: A Cross-Cultural Study"

Mary Daly, *Gyn/Ecology*

Sharon Lebell, *Naming Ourselves, Naming Our Children*

George Orwell, *1984*

Raphael Patai, *The Hebrew Goddess*
Joan Rockwell, *Fact in Fiction*
Rosemary Radford Ruether, ed., *Religion and Sexism*
Elizabeth Cady Stanton, *The Woman's Bible*

PREPARATION FOR THE NEXT SESSION

Remind participants of the readings for the next session. Ask them to think particularly about goals 1 to 3 for Session 7 and to keep these in mind as they do the assigned readings and as they observe the week's news and events in their own lives during the week.

CLOSING

As appropriate.

The transformation over time of the Great Goddess into Mary, mother of Jesus. This madonna and child, known as the "Vierge Ouvrante," was of painted wood, from fifteenth-century France. This is the figure closed. Its front is segmented into two doors. To provide an arresting leap ahead in time, these doors open to reveal a smaller scene of the later crucifixion of the man Jesus shown here as the child in his mother's arms. Line drawing from the original: John Mason.

From a medieval woodcut, 1555 A.D., showing the burning of three witches. The strange figure at the top of the picture is identified as that of the Devil claiming their souls. Particularly interesting is the fact that this Devil has breasts and a sepentine body. Again we find art used to sell and reinvorce the idea of woman as evil, and subliminally—as the snake was one of her epiphanies—to vilify and discredit the ancient Goddess. Line drawing from the original: Jeff Helwig.

Session 7:
The Quest for
Peace, Creativity, and
Partnership

GOALS

1. To take a fresh look at recorded history from a new perspective taking into account both halves of humanity (women and men) as well as the latest archeological discoveries about prehistoric societies such as Old Europe and Minoan Crete.

2. To reassess ideals and realities of democracy in ancient Greece and in the modern world from the perspective of the dominator and partnership models.

3. To gain new insights into Christianity—as it began and as it developed—from the consideration of the partnership-dominator dynamic.

4. To begin to allow ourselves to experience our own feelings of loss, anger, and grief, specifically in relation to our hidden partnership heritage and the way powerful stories and images have served to program our subconscious minds, often literally standing reality on its head.

READINGS

- *The Chalice and the Blade:*
    Chapter 8, "The Other Half of History: Part I"
    Chapter 9, "The Other Half of History: Part II"
    Chapter 10, "The Patterns of the Past: Gylany and History"

MATERIALS

Regular supplies (see Session 6's section on preparation for this session).

PREPARATION FOR FACILITATORS

Same as for Session 2.

GETTING STARTED

After opening the meeting as usual, you may want to proceed to a discussion of the insights members have had since the last meeting through their experiences and through the readings for this session. Ask each person to share an insight that relates specifically to goals 2 and 3 for this session: a new understanding of democracy and/or Christianity.

For example, the story by Augustine recounted on p. 114 in *The Chalice and the Blade* tells of how when Greek society shifted to descent traced through the father rather than the mother, Athenian women *lost* the right to vote. This casts a new light on the commonly held idea that Athens was the cradle of democracy. This in turn has interesting ramifications for the understanding of modern developments, such as the contemporary struggle of women for equal political rights and participation.

Another specific point is the new understanding we gain of prayer to the Catholic Virgin Mary as a reflection and also a co-option of prayer to the ancient Goddess. Again, the fact that "Mariology" came out of a period of strong gylanic resurgence (see Chapter 10 of *The Chalice and the Blade*) makes it easier to see how the contemporary surge of interest in the Goddess and the struggle of women to reenter the priesthood relates to the powerful contemporary partnership thrust.

You may want to imagine yourselves in an early Christian community where the deity was described as both Mother and Father and both women and men were leaders. You may also want to imagine what kinds of prayers were said. You could make up such a prayer or the key elements in it, perhaps beginning with "Our Holy Mother and Father, in thy love we trust."

FURTHER EXERCISES

At this point some members of the group might want to express their grief and/or anger about all that was lost in the shift from a partnership to a dominator direction, or to find some way to honor that heritage. One way of doing this is to ask the group to try to create a ritual in celebration of the Goddess or for personal healing.

A HEALING RITUAL

Vicki Noble's *Motherpeace*, Hallie Austin Iglehart's *Womanspirit*, and Starhawk's *The Spiral Dance* are useful sources of information on creating rituals. You might want to start with an invocation from Starhawk's adaptation of "Charge of the Star Goddess":

"I who am the beauty of the green earth and the white moon among the stars and the mysteries of the waters, I call upon your soul to arise and come unto Me. For I am the soul of Nature that gives life to the universe. From Me all things proceed and unto Me they must return. Let My worship be in the heart that rejoices, for behold—all acts of love and pleasure are my rituals."

Then the participants might want to share their feelings. Ask them to particularly comment on how it feels to have both women and men prepare and officiate at a ritual, rather than just having it done by men.

Living in a world where the focus is on only half of humanity— where women (or if it were a matriarchy, men) are by and large written out of what is considered important knowledge or information—is like walking around with blinders on. Use the following exercise to treat this subject more lightly.

A HALF-WORLD EXERCISE

Have the participants cover their eyes with one hand, leaving only a slight crack between two fingers over one eye to peer through.

Discuss the difference in what you see. Then walk around the room, trying to avoid bumping into one another. Report how soon you begin to adapt to this distortion—how soon you can perform adequately with an incomplete information base. Now take your hand away. How is our perception of reality distorted by limited perceptual input?

As in every session, the facilitators should use the newsprint pad to record the feelings and ideas shared by the members of the group.

DISCUSSION TOPICS

1. The terms *androcracy* and *gylany* are used to describe two different "attractors" affecting the dialectical movement between periods of greater creativity, peace, and equity on the one hand and times of heightened male dominance, repression, and warfare on the other.

   What are the implications of this periodic wave pattern for our present and future?

   How does looking at both halves of humanity (women and men) and the values stereotypically attributed to "femininity" and "masculinity" help us see the connections between:

   - rigid male dominance and war?
   - the patriarchal family structure and an authoritarian government?
   - a partnership family and real democracy?

2. Our primarily Western heritage is said to derive from ancient Greece and the Judeo-Christian tradition. Today, an even more ancient heritage is becoming apparent. Discuss the implications of these discoveries.

   In relation to ancient Greece, for example:

   - It has been suggested that the *Odyssey,* partly because it contains so many portraits of powerful female figures, was written by a woman. Do you think there may be merit to this theory? What elements of the *Odyssey* do you think reflect the author's wish to honor the earlier heritage where women were priestesses and practiced the esoteric arts of healing and magic? What parts of the *Odyssey* reflect the need in an already primarily dominator society to tell a story where only male warriors can be heroes? Could the author have been deliberately trying to sneak in some of the earlier mythology? Or could it have been primarily unconscious?

   - Explore possible connections between Catal Huyuk, Minoan Crete, and pre-Socratic Greece. What may link the three in terms of geography and settlement? In terms of belief systems and values? What is different?

   - Discuss the most compelling evidence of the mix of partnership and dominator cultures in ancient Greece. What are some elements of partnership culture? What are some elements of dominator culture?

   - What do you think of Aristophanes' satirical portrayal of an early women's peace movement in *Lysistrata*? If you are familiar with the play, you may want to discuss the use of trivialization and humor at the expense of women and compare with sexist, black, or other ethnic jokes.

   In relation to Christianity, the following questions may be of interest:

   - What do you think your reaction would be if the teachings about compassion, empathy (doing unto others as you would want them to do unto you), and nonviolence (turning the other cheek) attributed to Jesus were instead attributed to a woman? What would be your first reaction? How do you think others would react—all the way from prominent political and religious leaders to your neighbors?

- Consider the question of whether Mary Magdalene was really a prostitute. In the first printing of *The Chalice and the Blade* that was assumed, on the basis of the New Testament. But there is also the possibility that this was a strategic device for discrediting her as an important Christian leader (which we know she was from the "heretic" Gnostic gospels). Discuss the question of prostitution and whether it would exist in a society where sexual morality did not have a double standard for women and men. (It is interesting to note in this connection that Jesus' arrest seems to have been set up by his stopping the stoning to death of an "immoral" woman; and how he challenged the double standard by asking who was so faultless that he could cast the first stone.)

- Can you remember when you first noticed the contradictions between, on the one hand, what Jesus said and his life and, on the other hand, some of the teachings and practices of the organized Church and professed Christians? How did this recognition affect you? How long did it last? Were you given, or did you find, reasons to quickly overlook this contradiction?

- How are the persecution, death, and vilification of Hypatia (and the canonization of the man who instigated her killing) as well as the witch-hunts and burnings of millions of women (many of them healers and "wise women") paralleled by Moslem fundamentalists' torturing, raping, and killing "errant" women in Iran today (sometimes just women who dared to be unveiled)? How are they related to the burning of family planning clinics by Christian fundamentalists and other acts of violence against women in the United States today?

SUPPLEMENTARY READINGS

For full titles and citations, see the References at the end of this book.

Aristophanes, *Lysistrata*

Mary Beard, *Woman as a Force in History*

Elise Boulding, *The Underside of History*

Roy Chamberlin and Herman Feldman, eds., *The Dartmouth Bible*

Carol Christ and Judith Plaskow, *Womanspirit Rising*

Elisabeth Schüssler Fiorenza, *In Memory of Her*

Carol Gilligan, *In a Different Voice*

Edward Hussey, *The Pre-Socratics*

Ervin Laszlo, *Evolution*

David Loye and Riane Eisler, "Chaos and Transformation"

Kate Millett, *Sexual Politics*

Virginia Ramey Mollenkott, *Women, Men, and the Bible*

Elaine Pagels, *The Gnostic Gospels*

Plato, *The Republic*

John Mansley Robinson, *An Introduction to Early Greek Philosophers*

Betty and Theodore Roszak, "The Hard and the Soft"

Sappho, *Lyrics in the Original Greek*

G. Rattray Taylor, *Sex in History*

Monique Wittig, *Les Guerilleres*

PREPARATION FOR THE NEXT SESSION

Remind group members of the readings for the next session. Again, for those who do not have *The Partnership Way*, facilitators may need to hand out copies of "Six Contrasts Between the Dominator and Partnership Systems," "The Everyday Partnership Action Chart," and "Human Rights." Also, facilitators should put the "Six Contrasts Between the Dominator and Partnership Systems" on newsprint to put up at the next session.

CLOSING

As appropriate.

Woman and man breaking free of our Dominator past. This visualization involved the collaborative or "partnership" artwork of Jeff Helwig and John Thompson of Carmel and August Rodin, late of Paris, France. (Rodin's sculpture *The Prodigal Son* provided the lines for the male figure).

Session 8:
Breaking Free

GOALS

1. To examine the modern progressive movements from a new perspective—without separating "women's rights" from "human rights."
2. To examine the relationship between the "private sphere" of the family and the "public" or political world.
3. To review and consolidate our understanding of the six major elements of the partnership and the dominator systems and how these six elements affect our ability to develop creative win/win rather than win/lose (more often, in fact, lose/lose) solutions to problems.

SIX CONTRASTS BETWEEN THE DOMINATOR AND PARTNERSHIP SYSTEMS

DOMINATOR SYSTEM	PARTNERSHIP SYSTEM
Rigid male dominance in all areas of life (as well as "hard" or "masculine" social priorities).	Equal partnership between women and men in all areas of life (as well as elevation of "soft" or "feminine" values in social governance).
"Strong man" rule, or a generally hierarchic and authoritarian family and social structure (where obedience to orders is expected).	A more democratic and equalitarian family and social structure (where participatory decision making is expected).

113

DOMINATOR SYSTEM (*cont.*)

A high degree of institutionalized social violence (i.e., rape, wife beating, child abuse, war), that is required to impose and maintain rigid economic, social, and political rankings.

Emphasis on technologies of destruction and domination.

Conquest of nature.

Fear and scarcity as the primary motivators for work.

PARTNERSHIP SYSTEM (*cont.*)

More peaceful and mutually satisfying personal, community, and global relations based on interconnection (linking rather than ranking).

Emphasis on creative technologies that sustain and enhance life.

Respect for nature.

Stimulation of creativity, self development, group or team responsibility, and concern for the larger community (from local to planetary) as primary motivators for work.

MATERIALS

Regular supplies.

PREPARATION FOR FACILITATORS

Same as for Session 2.

READINGS

- *The Chalice and the Blade:*

    Chapter 11, "Breaking Free: The Unfinished Transformation"

- *The Partnership Way:*

    Riane Eisler, "Human Rights: Toward an Integrated Theory for Action"

    "The Partnership and Dominator Models" (Basic Configuration and How to Recognize)

    "The Everyday Partnership Action Chart"

GETTING STARTED

This session takes us squarely into present time, into our modern world and the crises and opportunities we face. It focuses on creative partnership alternatives to the dominator model.

After the usual opening, you may want to start by putting up the six major elements of the partnership and dominator systems on newsprint for discussion and review.

FURTHER EXERCISES

The following exercise relates to "The Partnership and Dominator Models" on pp. 179–90 in the Partnership Resources.

FROM DOMINATION TO PARTNERSHIP

In this exercise, the session facilitator divides a large page of newsprint into three columns, headed "The Dominator Way," at the top of the left column, "The Partnership Way," at the top of the middle column, and "Action," at the top of the right column.

The participants are asked to give examples of contrasting dominator and partnership characteristics, attitudes, and behaviors in all aspects of life, from political and work relations to woman-man relations and child rearing. Then participants are asked to give examples from their own experience, observation, and/or creative thinking of specific ways to shift from the dominator to the partnership model. See the "Everyday Partnership Action Chart" in Partnership Resources for examples to get the group started.

During this exercise, keep the following in mind:

- Try to avoid slipping into a polemical ("us against them") stance and to remind ourselves that we have all learned dominator behaviors, that we are all to varying degrees still conditioned by a world that is oriented more to the dominator than to the partnership model.

- Point out that a partnership society is *not* a society devoid of conflict. As is brought out in Chapter 13 of *The Chalice and the Blade,* the dominator system *suppresses* conflict—even though conflict is natural since people have different needs, desires, and aspirations. By contrast, the partnership system recognizes conflict and does not suppress it (so that it does not have to take recourse to violence and other extremes). Rather, it deals with conflict creatively, and trains both women and men to do this (this is exemplified by the current trend toward exploring new methods for nonviolent conflict resolution).

- Stress that the partnership society is *not* a leaderless, laissez-faire, or unstructured society. As many of the experiences of people in the 1960s show, such an approach does *not* work. There are leaders in both a dominator and a partnership society. But since power is defined very differently, so is leadership.

    In the dominator model, power is defined as "power over" and leadership is equated with control. In the partnership model, power is viewed primarily as "power to" or "power with" (*actualizing* rather than dominating power). And leadership is equated with the ability to bring forth from others their highest creativity and effectiveness in furthering mutually agreed upon goals.

- It is interesting that this partnership view of leadership is gaining currency in many corporations today, because it leads to higher productivity along with greater job satisfaction. It is also interesting, though rarely noted, that this enabling and more empathic style of leadership often comes very easily to women, as women's socialization has stereotypically stressed the enabling or nurturing of others along with empathy for them. Similarly, in the corporate sector, cooperative teamwork where workers participate in decision making is gaining recognition as a more productive as well as a more enjoyable way of functioning.

- Finally, a partnership society is not to be confused with a utopian or unattainably "ideal" society. Rather, it is a viable alternative to the dominator model—one that guided our social development in the mainstream of our original cultural evolution, and one that is today reemerging more powerfully than ever before in recorded history. Most important, it is a model that requires all of our active cocreation, our commitment to making the personal and social changes that can make it a reality.

DISCUSSION TOPICS

1. The conventional view is grounded in concepts of capitalism vs. communism, extreme right vs. extreme left, developed countries vs. developing countries, religion vs. secularism, East vs. West, etc. This has produced a high degree of fragmentation and confusion. From the perspective of the contrast between the dominator and partnership models, we can see that the underlying struggle is between these two different possibilities for our society. Using the six major elements of each model (see "Six Contrasts"), reexamine these conventional polarities.

    The following are some possible questions:

    -   What are the similarities between Khomeini's Iran, P. W. Botha's South Africa, and the vision of the United States proposed by men such as Jerry Falwell? What are the differences?

    -   What do abolitionism, pacifism, anarchism, anticolonialism, and environmentalism have in common?

    -   What does feminism have in common with these movements? In what regard does it differ?

    -   What does Chapter 11 of *The Chalice and the Blade* suggest to you about the theoretical and practical pros and cons of capitalism? Of socialism? Of communism?

    -   How do you think "progressive" ideas such as progress, equality, and freedom might have been received by the Kurgan invaders? How would the "Fathers" of the orthodox Church who allied themselves with the Emperor Constantine have received these ideas?

    -   What do you think are the major similarities and differences between the Kurgans and the Nazis?

    -   Do punk rock and religious fundamentalism have anything in common? Do these trends represent ways of trying to escape the challenge of transformation?

- What do you think are the implications of the idea that the "modern gylanic thrust may be seen as an adaptive process impelled by the survival impulse of our species"?

2. The international human rights movement was an outgrowth of the eighteenth-century "rights of man" philosophies of thinkers like Locke and Rousseau. In that same century, Mary Wollstonecraft and other thinkers brought up the issue of the rights of women. By the nineteenth century, feminist philosophy was an important cultural strain—but one still generally relegated to the intellectual ghetto of the "woman question." This splitting off or peripheralizing of the question of the rights of one half of humanity (actually the numerical majority) from the mainstream of progressive thought has undermined social and cultural progress, so that almost every step forward has been followed by a regressive step back. Discuss ways to heal this fundamental internal inconsistency in progressive thought and action. Some possible focusing questions:

   - How do dominator thought and action (on the right or on the left) integrate the so-called public and private spheres?

   - How does the family serve as a microcosm of and training ground for social, political, and economic relations?

   - Why was defeating the Equal Rights Amendment to the U.S. Constitution a top agenda item for the American right while its passage was only a secondary or "women's issue" for the liberals and the left?

   - How is women's contemporary struggle for reproductive freedom related to human rights? To social and cultural progress? To human survival?

   - What can we do to support women in the Third World struggling against laws that still sanction wife beating and genital mutilation?

   - What can we do about all laws that rigidly define and impose a secondary social status on women?

   - How can we together construct and disseminate an integrated new progressive partnership ideology?

3. What does psychologist David Winter's study of Don Juan (discussed in Chapter 10 of *The Chalice and the Blade*) tell us

about the modern fascination with James Bond–type movies and sex/killing films such as *Psycho* and *Snuff*? How do books such as Kate Millett's *Sexual Politics* further illuminate this problem? How do stories, movies, and scientific studies of equal partnership between women and men strengthen the movement toward a more peaceful and creative world based primarily on affiliation rather than violent confrontation and domination?

4. Discuss how the structure of the workplace is affected by the dominator and partnership models respectively.

   • How do you think the first factories might have been designed if a partnership rather than a dominator model of society had been in place during the Industrial Revolution?

   • Would sweatshops and assembly lines, where workers became cogs in a machine, have been built?

   • How do you think the contemporary partnership trends in the workplace, such as parental leave, attention to day care for children, job sharing, flex time, and other social inventions that stem from an integrated female/male workplace/home partnership approach relate to other social trends?

   • How can they be supported and accelerated?

5. The current struggle over comparable worth is basically a struggle over what kind of work should be socially (and thus also monetarily) rewarded.

   • What is the intrinsic difference between plumbing repair (which is highly paid) and child care (which is one of the lowest paid professions)? Which one has more social value?

   • How do you think our economic models can be modified so that activities conventionally considered "women's work" can be properly valued and rewarded in terms of status and pay?

SUPPLEMENTARY READINGS

For full titles and citations, see the References at the end of this book.

Riane Eisler and David Loye, "The 'Failure' of Liberalism"
Ronald Fletcher, "The Making of the Modern Family"
Erich Fromm, *Escape from Freedom*
Robert Heilbroner, *The Worldly Philosophers*
Sonia Johnson, *From Housewife to Heretic*
David Loye, *The Healing of a Nation*
Karl Marx and Friedrich Engels, *The Communist Manifesto*
Kate Millett, *Sexual Politics*
Robin Morgan, ed., *Sisterhood Is Global*
Isolina Ricci, *Mom's House, Dad's House*
Miriam Schneir, ed., *Feminism: The Essential Historical Writings*
Dale Spender, *Feminist Theorists*
Gloria Steinem, *Outrageous Acts and Everyday Rebellions*

PREPARATION FOR THE NEXT SESSION

Remind group members of the readings for the next session. Ask them to make lists of all the books they own or they can think of that support the androcratic system. Do the same for the gylanic system. Bring these lists to the next meeting for discussion.

CLOSING

As appropriate.

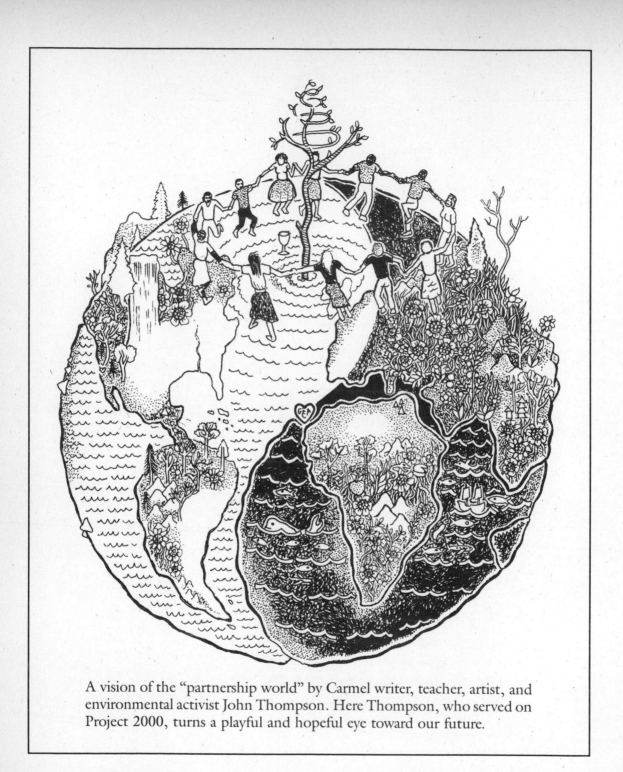

A vision of the "partnership world" by Carmel writer, teacher, artist, and
environmental activist John Thompson. Here Thompson, who served on
Project 2000, turns a playful and hopeful eye toward our future.

Session 9:
The Evolutionary Crossroads

GOALS

1. To consolidate our understanding of how many of our personal problems are symptoms of an unhealthy and imbalanced social body.
2. To explore how the global threats of totalitarianism, overpopulation, environmental pollution, and nuclear holocaust relate to stereotypical roles of women and men.
3. To review the cultural transformation theory introduced in *The Chalice and the Blade*.
4. To share our hopes and plans for a partnership future.
5. To explore the possibility of individual and/or group partnership action projects.

READINGS

- *The Chalice and the Blade:*

    Chapter 12, "The Breakdown of Evolution: A Dominator Future"

    Chapter 13, "Breakthrough in Evolution: Toward a Partnership Future"

    Review pp. xv–xxiii (from the introduction); pp. 104–6 (on linking and ranking as well as the difference between actualization and domination hierarchies); and pp. 135–37 and pp. 147–55 (on cultural transformation theory)

- *The Partnership Way:*
  Riane Eisler, "Technology at the Turning Point"
  Review all Dominator and Partnership charts and text.

MATERIALS

Regular supplies.

PREPARATION FOR FACILITATORS

Same as for Session 2.

GETTING STARTED

After the customary opening, the cofacilitators may want to ask each of the participants to share briefly with the group what they think is the most important thing they have gained from the meetings. This is summarized on newsprint by the cofacilitators.

Another way to begin this future-oriented discussion might be to go around the room and ask the participants to share briefly with the group the feelings evoked for them by the closing passage from *The Chalice and the Blade* and, equally important, actions that they think can help translate it into reality.

CLOSING PASSAGE FROM
THE CHALICE AND THE BLADE

"For above all, this gylanic world will be a world where the minds of children—both girls and boys—will no longer be fettered. It will be a world where limitation and fear will no longer be systematically taught us through myths about how inevitably evil and perverse we humans are. In this world, children will not be taught epics about men who are honored for being violent or fairy tales about children who are lost in frightful woods where women are malevolent witches. They will be taught new myths, epics, and stories in which human beings are good; men are peaceful; and the power of creativity and love—symbolized by the sacred Chalice, the holy vessel of life—is the governing principle. For in this gylanic world, our drive for justice, equality, and freedom, our thirst for knowledge and spiritual illumination, and our yearning for love and beauty will at last be freed. And after the bloody detour of androcratic history, both women and men will at last find out what being human can mean."

After some discussion, facilitators should bring the group focus to the question of how the participants think they can best apply what they have gained from these sessions *to their own lives*. This is a continuation of the work of the last session, using the charts on pp. 179–87 as working models. But it takes the process one step further—to an exploration of individual and/or group partnership *action projects*.

FURTHER EXERCISES

Some of the group members will want to continue to meet. Others may not find this possible or may not be interested. But people in groups who have shared important experiences often want to remain in touch. And specific partnership action projects can now provide the logical next step. As a result of these weeks of joint exploration, members of the group now have the information base for effective personal and social transformation. Now is the time to try out this new knowledge with a specific action project.

To prompt discussion, you may want to ask:

- What are the best opportunities for partnership social action that lie close at hand in our lives? In our own community?
- What are some specific actions that can help heal the wounds we all carry from dominator child raising and other dominator social interactions?
- How can we most effectively demonstrate in our own lives that the personal *is* political?

DEVELOPING PARTNERSHIP ACTION PROJECTS

To develop a partnership action project, through discussion decide on a specific area to focus on. For example, the human rights article in Partnership Resources suggests that laws can be important vehicles for accelerating partnership change. The technology article (pp. 213–24) in Partnership Resources stresses the essential role of the media of communication. This entails not just recognizing how dominator myths have held us back, but most urgently, the creation of alternative stories and images of partnership.

Here are some specific ideas.

Media Action

Social observers increasingly recognize how much of what we see in films and on TV reinforces destructive attitudes and behaviors. The barrage of "fun" violence, mechanical, conquest-oriented sex, and the consumerization of all aspects of human interaction serve to deny the reality both of human suffering and of joy. Perhaps most insidious is how this deadening of our emotions through one rapid fragmentized image after another deadens our sense of empathy, even for ourselves.

The sheer mass and frequency of negative images—of "fun" violence, of bad news, of sitcoms based on "hilarious" insensitivity and manipulativeness—also serves another key dominator purpose. It keeps us trapped in an escapist mode.

In short, even when mass media programs are not blatant dominator propaganda (as in the idealization of a James Bond or Rambo male and the presentation of women as the violent hero's prizes), they communicate a basic sense of powerlessness, indeed of hopelessness: a message that everything is trivial and that there is nothing to do about it except vicariously to "enjoy" an essentially meaningless ride until we die.

Call yourselves the Partnership Media Action Group. Print yourselves an impressive letterhead and elect officers. Look for the good articles and shows that express partnership themes. They do appear—all the time! Collaborate in writing letters of *praise* to the writers, producers, network, local newspaper, sponsors—whoever and whatever will encourage more of this. Creative media people who stick out their necks to do good things *need your support*—and *groups* can have much greater impact than individuals.

Art Action

The same dominator messages that ruin so much of the media also provide the underlying message of much of modern art. The currently fashionable deconstructionism, parodying a despised materialistic mass culture, is underneath its veneer of social criticism another means of asserting that nothing can be done. It assumes that the only role for the artist is that of disenchanted, indeed disgusted, observer and that the only function of art is as a social mirror, a reflection of an alienating, fragmenting, and often horrifying but essentially empty reality.

Such assumptions serve to maintain the dominator system. Fortunately, there are more and more artists who understand that the *deconstruction* of conventional images is only the first step, that it is merely a door to the next step: the *reconstruction* of "reality" through new/old mythic images and stories.* As artist and writer Suzi Gablik notes, the partnership art movement is "reconstructionism"—as reconstructive artists embrace the challenge and responsibility of being "orchestrators of culture and consciousness."

Bring together several local artists whose work seems to express partnership art. Get them to read *The Chalice and the Blade*—or any good summary—and then work with them to define for yourselves what partnership art is. Next, identify more local "partnership" artists using these criteria, and then work with a good local art gallery to stage your own pioneering partnership art exhibit. (A "Partnership and the Arts" concept paper can be obtained from the Center for Partnership Studies.)

Education Action

Art, the media, education—these are prime vehicles that each of us can and must use. We can do this by individually and jointly working to ensure that the conventional dominator images and stories are gradually crowded out by new/old partnership images and stories.

---

*We are indebted to Suzi Gablik for the term *reconstruction* as a description of the major artistic movement that, as she writes in her forthcoming book *The Reenchantment of Art*, has a key role to play in "accelerating the transformation from a dominator to a partnership culture in all aspects of our lives."

Another good project is the joint redesign of course curricula at all educational levels in areas ranging all the way from history and social science to art and religious studies. The need for partnership materials is urgent, and every one of us can contribute.

If you have a knack for drawing, you might try your hand at children's picture books, posters, or cartoons. Whatever the area, work with sympathetic teachers with experience in building—or, often, having to just carry out—curricula in your area of interest. When you've got a product that looks good, give it exposure through talks to open-minded PTAs, school superintendents, and school board members.

Economic Action

For those who are interested in positive changes in the corporate, government, and nonprofit employment sector, the focus for a partnership action project could be how the redesign of the workplace and the movement toward a partnership family go hand in hand. For example, if men are to share with women the caring for and nurturing of children, parental leaves and on-site child care are required.

There is also the critical issue of comparable worth, of adequate pay and recognition of work stereotypically associated with women. Since this work is often the work of caring for the needs of others (as in child care or the caretaking of the elderly), its devaluation has very negative socio-economic consequences for us all.

For example, politicians find it difficult to justify budgets that allocate significant sums to "welfare" services—or caring for others—as many of their constituents do not think that caring for people's welfare is economically valuable. Similarly, since women are stereotypically associated with cleaning up the family's living quarters, corporations do not give high value (or sufficient funding) to cleaning up industrial waste in our national and global living quarters.

A partnership action project would be geared to designing and presenting programs to educate people about these issues. Such a project would also raise awareness about a point stressed in both the human rights article and Chapters 11 and 13 of *The Chalice and the Blade*: there is a need for moving from the male as the norm (whether in the design of cars, factories, or religious and political institutions) to a new gender-holistic or partnership model. In other words, it means leaving behind the stereotypes and paying attention to the real needs of *both* girls and boys, women and men, for a family and work environment that supports and enhances everyone's well-being, productivity, and creativity.

Environmental Action

The mix of the dominator model and high technology is at the root of our growing environmental crisis. Certainly action is essential to raise consciousness about rain forests (the lungs of our planet), the health risk of pollution and holes in the ozone layer, saving dolphins, and resource depletion through wasteful overconsumption. But as long as the notion of humans' right (and need) to dominate and conquer nature prevails, we are like the legendary boy putting his finger in the hole in the dike. What is needed is a fundamental shift in consciousness about the connectedness or linking of all life forms on this planet and our responsibility in our cultural and technological evolution to act in harmony with nature, rather than just to exploit it. And here is where partnership education—including knowledge of the old mythology about the Earth as our mother—comes in.

A specific example of how this new/old story can be communicated relates to the dolphin and the ancient Minoans, who lived in more harmonious partnership with one another and with nature. They felt so connected with the dolphin that it is frequently portrayed in their art. A vivid example, which could be reproduced for a Partnership Ecology education project, is the beautiful dolphin fresco in the Palace at Knossos—which looks remarkably like a three thousand-year-old precursor of a modern ecology poster. Showing how what we call our ecological consciousness is rooted in ancient traditions can greatly accelerate its acceptance.

In more affluent nations such as the United States, which consumes a disproportionate percentage of the world's resources,

Modern ecololgy poster? What we think of as ecological consciousness is visible in this thirty-five-hundred-year-old fresco from Crete. Line drawing from the original: Jim Beeman.

overconsumption and wastefulness are major ecological issues, as they contribute to both natural resources depletion and such environmental health hazards as our mountains of toxic waste. One of the reasons people overconsume is that this serves as a substitute for the self-esteem and satisfying interpersonal relationships that are so difficult to build in a dominator-oriented society. Therefore another basic element in ecology education is to help people see these connections more clearly. This could help to counterbalance the false promises of ads that literally create addictions to unnecessary and often even harmful purchasing and overconsumption. An important byproduct of such a partnership education project would be the freeing of time, energy, and money to focus, not on more material accumulations, but on the only accumulations that are truly lasting: our human relations and our human development, both individually and socially.

Personal Action and Community Building

Remember, a group begins with two. You might choose a personal project, such as the creation of a partnership relationship with someone you live with. Keep a progress journal to review together. Or together carry out research, like making a list of partnership literature, movies, or TV programs, and disseminate it through schools, churches, and other organizations.

Again, we are here dealing with action linked to fundamental changes in consciousness. In psychological terms, it means moving from a defense-needs to a growth-needs motivational system where fear (and hence the "need" to control) is not paramount. It takes us full circle to the question of the basic obstacles to partnership between women and men, women and women, men and men, children and children, children and parents—and between nations and nations. It also means taking an even closer look at the prison of the "macho" role, which goes along with the manipulative and subtly controlling and devious female stereotype of the "Total Woman," both of which keep us locked in the "war of the sexes" and its corollaries, warfare and the conquest of nature.

Another personal action project would be to have the members of this group commit to form an ongoing personal and family support system. This is not a new partnership idea, as it has been an important component in many social movements, from Quakers to women's support groups. It is a very effective and practical way of providing concrete personal and family support, such as helping to care for one another's children and bringing food and medicine if someone is sick. It is also a very effective means of partnership community building. These local partnership communities could eventually come together and form national and international communities of mutual encouragement and support. Such links with like-minded and like-hearted individuals and families are wonderful as a way of enriching our lives and feeling more comfortable and secure, for example, if one is traveling. Most important, they can be the basis for concerted and lasting social action and positive change.

For other ideas, see "Partnership Action: A Quick Guide" in Additional Exercises and Topics for Discussion.

Political Action

We have stressed in both *The Chalice and the Blade* and in this book that the personal *is* political, that what we do in our personal lives is inextricably connected with the larger, so-called public sphere. However, we have also brought out time and time again that to heal ourselves we have to heal society. In other words, without fundamental changes in belief systems, laws, policies, and institutions our personal healing can go only so far and no further.

Perhaps nowhere is this as apparent as in the relationship between public policies and laws, economic and social development, and the tremendous obstacles to improving the quality of life—indeed, all too often to saving lives—in the Third World. Moreover, on our planet—so shrunken by incredibly powerful technologies of communication and transportation, as well as destruction—what happens to people in the Third World profoundly affects our own chances for personal growth and even survival.

In Chapter 12 of *The Chalice and the Blade,* the relationship between war and peace, ecological balance or imbalance, and so-called women's issues is discussed and the point is made that the kinds of policies required to maintain a dominator/androcratic system are on a potentially lethal collision course with the policies that can lead to a sustainable and vastly improved future.

The most urgent case in point is the policies required to deal with the global population explosion that poses a massive threat not only to the quality of all of our lives but to our very survival as a species on our planet.

In Additional Exercises and Topics, you will find "Women, Development, and Population: Highlights from the 1989 State of World Population Report" by Dr. Nafis Sadik, executive director of the United Nations Population Fund, which more than any previous United Nations document on the subject clearly shows the essential link between raising the status of Third World women and economic and social development for all. This important document makes specific recommendations that could be the inspiration and basis for political action projects.

You may want to construct your own project to support Third World women's efforts to gain more equal partnership with men. This could be a local project, a national project, or an international project. You may want to design and implement your own project or you may want to support existing projects. For example, the Katalysis and the Earth Trust Foundation support a project modeled on the Grameen Bank Project successfully used in Bangladesh that donates relatively small sums of money to women in Third World villages for them to administer as bankers who, in turn, make small loans to women for various productive and beneficial projects and enterprises. And women's world banking and the global fund for women make larger loans and grants. Or you may want to concentrate your efforts on educating our policymakers since U.S. aid projects can be exponentially more effective once they recognize the centrality of women to economic, social, and political progress.

If the group—or part of it—wants to launch its own partnership action project, discussion and planning will likely take up most of the remaining time for this closing session.

If, however, all or part of the group wants to continue discussions based on the book—with the idea of an action project later—the following topics can be used in continuing discussions beyond this closing session. See also Additional Exercises and Topics for Discussion in this book.

TOPICS FOR CONTINUING DISCUSSION

1. We know that by reexamining our personal and family history we can begin to change unhealthy habits of functioning. We are now also learning that many painful habits are the result of having had to function in a dominator system.

   What are the implications of a dominator system for our self-image and self-esteem as women and men?

   • How does the sense of failure experienced by many men relate to the stereotypical expectations of the male role as being one of one-upmanship: of sexual "scoring," of "winning" or "losing" in the workplace, of always being in control?

- How do women's well-known problems with self-esteem relate to the still-prevalent myths about female sinfulness, inferiority, and untrustworthiness?

- What are the implications of the dominator system for our family relations? For example, how does what we today call codependency or addiction to abusive and unhealthy relationships (where an individual seeks to manipulate or placate an abusive family member) relate to the stereotypical passive feminine role in a dominator family? How do men's familiar problems with forming intimate relations relate to the stereotypical image of the "strong" or "macho" man?

- What are the implications of the dominator system for race relations? For example, how are the myths of the "happy nigger" and the "contented housewife" related? How are South African apartheid and the rigid segregation of women in fundamentalist Muslim regimes such as Khomeini's Iran related?

2. One of the major themes of Chapter 12 is the impossibility of implementing the kinds of policies that can effectively counter the global threats of totalitarianism, overpopulation, environmental pollution, and nuclear holocaust while attempting to maintain a dominator system founded on the stereotypical male/female roles. How do you think both the general public and policymakers can quickly be made aware of this critical issue? The following questions may be helpful in exploring this area.

- How do you think world hunger, malnutrition, desertification, low levels of competency and education, and other pressing problems of development and survival would be affected by an approach to global development in which women's needs and aspirations were central rather than peripheral? (Chapter 12 of *The Chalice and the Blade, Women in Poverty,* edited by Devaki Jain and Nirmala Bannerjee, and the human rights article by Riane Eisler reprinted in the Partnership Resources section may be particularly relevant here.)

- Why do so many people (including scientists and other experts) express such grave concerns about the population explosion, mounting ecological disasters, the threat of economic collapse, etc., while others predict only minimal problems that will by and large take care of themselves?

- How do you think this relates to the mixed dominator and partnership messages received from politicians and the media?

- How do you feel about the United States government's official abandonment during the 1980s of a world leadership role in population control, family planning, equal rights for women, ecological protection, and the exploration of solar power and other decentralizing alternatives to nuclear power?

- What feelings, thoughts, and possible actions are evoked in you by the statement that "a dominator future is sooner or later almost certainly a future of global nuclear war—and the end of all of humanity's problems and aspirations"?

3. Some theoretical issues may bear clarification. For example:

- How does the cultural transformation theory differ from the conventional linear or straight-line stages of cultural evolution approach?

- How would you describe the difference between actualization and domination hierarchies?

- How do you see the relationship between "productive" and "destructive" approaches to conflict in terms of Jean Baker Miller's analysis?

- How would you describe alternative views of power in terms of concepts such as win/win and win/lose, or of Jean Baker Miller's differentiation of "power for oneself" from "power over others"?

- How would you describe partnership healing? How does it differ from many conventional approaches? Can you think of specific instances of both types and of ways to encourage the growth of partnership healing?

- What does the phrase "alienation of caring labor" mean to you?

- How can we use technology to accelerate the shift from domination to partnership?
- How can we use the media? (The technology article on pp. 213–24 may help stimulate this discussion.)
- How can we use the political process?
- How can we involve the corporate sector?
- How can we work through our churches and other religious institutions?

SUPPLEMENTARY READINGS

For full titles and citations, see the References at the end of this book.

Lester R. Brown, *State of the World 1988*
Helen Caldicott, *Nuclear Madness*
Fritjof Capra, *The Turning Point*
Rachel Carson, *Silent Spring*
Charlotte Perkins Gilman, *Herland*
Bertram Gross, *Friendly Fascism*
Hazel Henderson, *The Politics of the Solar Age*
Perdita Huston, *Third World Women Speak Out*
Devaki Jain and Nirmala Bannerjee, eds., *Women in Poverty*
Ervin Laszlo, *Evolution*
David Loye, *The Sphinx and the Rainbow*
John McHale, *The Future of the Future*
Jean Baker Miller, *Toward a New Psychology of Women*
Hilkka Pietila, *Tomorrow Begins Today*
Betty Reardon, *Sexism and the War System*
Jonas Salk, *Anatomy of Reality*
Gita Sen, *Development Crises and Alternative Visions*
Ruth Sivard, *World Military and Social Expenditures*
Charlene Spretnak and Fritjof Capra, *Green Politics*
Robert Theobald, *The Rapids of Change*

CLOSING

The main thing to accomplish in this last session is to leave everyone with a good feeling about themselves, their partners in this new learning experience, and new prospects for a better future.

If the group, or any part of it, is ready to launch a partnership action project, be sure responsibility for this project is in specific hands—newly elected facilitators, or yourselves, if you wish to continue with such a project. Having gained this valuable experience as partnership discussion group facilitators, however, you may be better off starting another discussion group and encouraging others to spin off action projects—until you're ready to switch roles, for a change. In any case, details such as meeting place and time for a spin-off action project should be decided upon before you part. If the group, or any part of it, wants to continue discussions before considering a partnership action project, see that this, too, is properly arranged.

You may want to end with some memorable ritual, visualization, or quiet time, but be sure to make it brief. The main thing you want to encourage is the feeling—and expression of this feeling—that over the past few weeks you have participated in a meaningful partnership, an exploration of a new future. And now the task is to work together toward this much better future with hope, with joy, and with a new conviction that it *can* be ours.

The reconstruction of our belief systems and institutions from a dominator to a partnership culture is in the hands of every one of us. These sessions have provided us with some tools for creative thinking and specific ways of empowering ourselves. Now is the time for action, for personal and social transformation—and it starts with each of us!

A NOTE TO FACILITATORS

Please send a summary of your group's collective comments and suggestions plus brief summaries of the results of the meetings to us at the Center for Partnership Studies, Box 51936, Pacific Grove, CA 93950.

This is a figure of the Goddess found on a gold pendant in Crete, dating back to 1500 B.C. Her headdress is of papyrus symbolizing the life-giving and sustaining powers of nature. Line drawing from the original: John Mason.

Additional Exercises
and Topics for
Discussion

Our Real History

contributed by Linda Grover
Klamath Falls, Oregon

I have found the following figures to be an effective way to get across the basic message of *The Chalice and the Blade*. They can be drawn on a blackboard or on a large newsprint pad, projected while you talk, or used as handouts.

Figure 1 shows at a glance the big picture, in terms of prehistory and history and female and male. Figure 2 shows where so much of what makes us human *really* comes from. Figure 3 shows our potential for change.

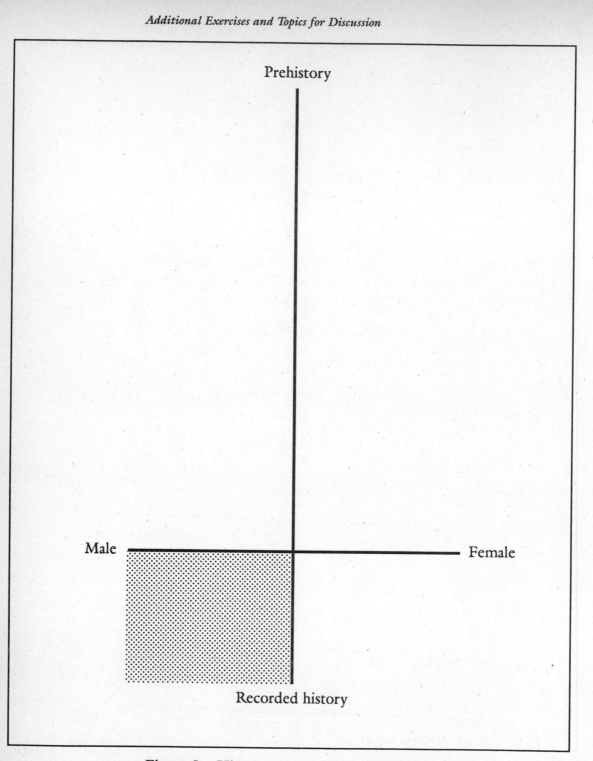

Figure 1. History as we learn it (shaded area).

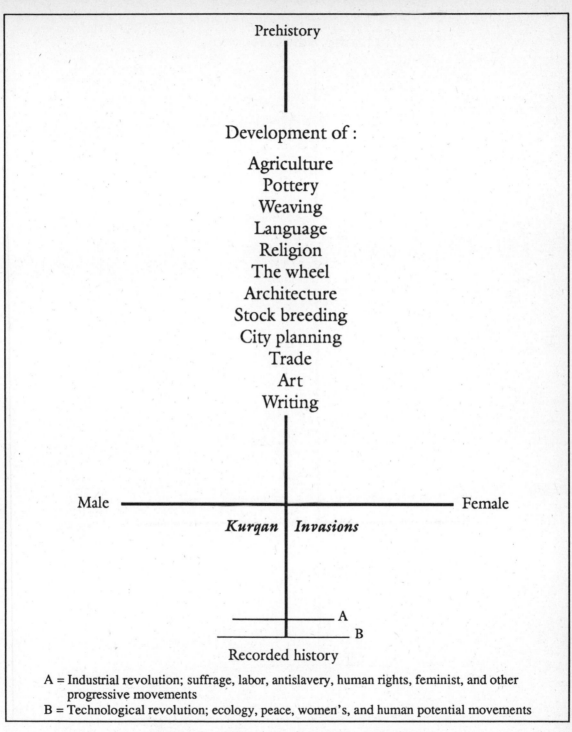

Figure 2. Who really did what—and when.

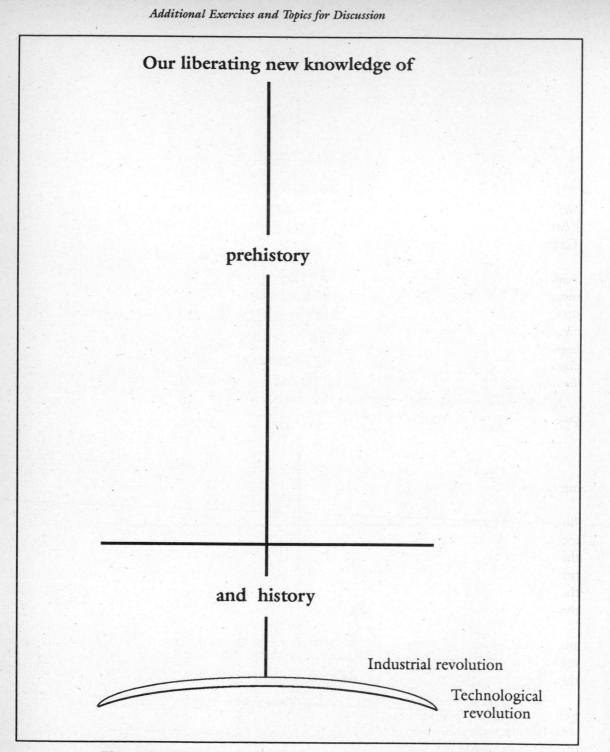

Figure 3. History as we would learn it in a partnership world.

Group Juggling

contributed by Carol Haag and Jennifer Macleod
Princeton Junction, New Jersey

This game has been used in training sessions for the Delaware-Raritan Girl Scout Council, Girl Scout troop events, church picnics, peace fairs, etc. It is based on a game reported in More New Games *by Andrew Fluegelman (Garden City, NY: Dolphin/Doubleday, 1981).*

This game is something to keep in mind when people say there is no such thing as a noncompetitive game that is enjoyable and also promotes healthful exercise, improves and provides practice in physical and mental skills and coordination, and improves and provides practice in the skills and rewards of cooperative action. Just as long as people don't think that now we've got to have Group Juggling competititve teams, high-pressure coaches, elaborate scoring systems, elimination tournaments, and big prizes for the winners and semi-disgrace for the losers!

Equipment needed: a few people, a few balls (preferably soft), and some space; the game can be adjusted to suit the space available.

Group juggling is a game in which people who may not be able to juggle individually can juggle through cooperating.

Everyone forms a circle and raises one hand. One person (the "initiator") takes a ball and throws it to someone else in the circle. The receiver notes who threw it to her, lowers her raised hand, and throws the ball to another person who has a raised hand. This process continues until everyone in the circle has received the ball at least once and the last throw goes back to the initiator—who continues the process by throwing it to the same person as before.

People should watch the person from whom they receive the ball and then throw it each time to the same person they did in the initial round. If a ball drops, the person nearest to it simply picks it up and throws to the person to whom she always throws.

Continue for a few rounds, until all is going smoothly. The initiator now adds a *second* ball. When that is also going smoothly (along with the first), she adds a *third* ball, and then a *fourth*—and as many as the group can keep going.

The group can go for

- the highest possible number of balls in the air,
- precision of throwing so none collide in mid-air and escape,
- the most hilarity as balls careen off each other crazily,
- the greatest speed, or
- nothing but the fun of creating something marvelous together.

The game is over when people are laughing too much to throw anything, or when it becomes boring and time for a new game.

The game can be modified for little children by sitting on the floor and rolling large balls—collisions are guaranteed. People who are good throwers can use hard balls and a large outdoor field. Mixed groups or "klutzes" can use Nerf balls, which are easily caught and incapable of injuring even the most unwary receiver.

Partnership Action: A Quick Guide

contributed by Gail Van Buuren
Pacific Grove, California

LIVING PARTNERSHIP

- Actively use partnership in your daily actiities and relationships.
- Introduce partnership concepts in your workplace, your club, your family.

STARTING GROUPS

- Plan a partnership evening with friends.
- Start a partnership group in your community.
- Become the facilitator of a workshop or partnership evening using *The Partnership Way* to explore partnership living.

SPEAKING AND WRITING

- Speak at meetings, clubs, church groups about any aspect of the transformation from domination to partnership.
- Speak to your schools about textbook updates incorporating a more balanced picture of our past and present.
- Give a guest talk in your child's or friend's classroom.
- Write letters to newspaper and magazine editors, TV and radio stations about the partnership movement; request they cover news everywhere expressing this new orientation to peace, ecology, economics, feminism—and all other aspects of our lives!

TEACHING

- Plan to teach a course on partnership—*The Partnership Way* will provide most of what you need to plan curricula.

- Influence others to do the same, particularly friends who are already teaching in schools, colleges, universities, and religious institutions.

RECREATING IN PARTNERSHIP

- Find or design cooperative as opposed to competitive games for children and/or adults to play and learn from.
- Create partnership literature for children and adults.
- Communicate the partnership model through your artistic medium.

SHARING *THE CHALICE AND THE BLADE*

- Give the book as a gift—the red and gold cover with Goddess figure is bright and festive for all occasions.
- Send a copy to the influential people to whom you have access, including corporation executives, politicians, teachers, ministers, and media people.
- Make sure that the book is available in school and public libraries and bookstores near you.
- Do the same with its companion discussion/action guide, *The Partnership Way.*

SUPPORTING THE CENTER FOR PARTNERSHIP STUDIES

- When speaking to groups, teaching a course, writing to the media, or just talking to friends and business associates, tell people about the Center for Partnership Studies.
- Do a fundraiser and send us an appropriate share.

GIVING US FEEDBACK

- Document what you are doing and send us summaries of what works.

- Let us know what aspects of *The Chalice and the Blade, The Partnership Way,* and the Center for Partnership Studies you find most important and/or useful.

Center for Partnership Studies, Box 51936, Pacific Grove, CA 93950.

Mindfulness Exercises

contributed by Ron Kurtz
Ashland, Oregon

These are exercises developed by Ron Kurtz, originator of Hakomi Therapy and author of the book by the same title, for a joint workshop he gave with Riane Eisler at Esalen in 1989. Ron can be reached at Hakomi of Ashland, P.O. Box 537, Ashland, OR 97520.

EXERCISE 1: MINDFULNESS FANTASY

The following fantasy is led by the facilitator. The purpose is to help participants to experience a clear, calm state of mindfulness to be used in other exercises that require mindfulness.

In a slow, soft voice, the facilitator speaks as follows:

Please allow yourself to come to a calm, quiet space inside yourself. Let the concerns of the day subside for now. As you are relaxing, I would like to guide you with some imagery. Imagine you and me sitting quietly by a still pond deep in a forest on a clear, comfortable day. We've been sitting for a long time, silently, without needing to speak. Just being quiet, feeling the air, soft and pleasant against the skin, with the smells of the forest around us. The forest is very still, except for the sounds of an occasional bird and only the slightest movement of the air. The face of the pond is still, the surface, mirrorlike. In that mirror we can see still clouds. Shifting focus, we can look through the mirror, seeing the pebbles at the bottom of the pond. As we're sitting, not speaking, you notice a leaf that's being carried by the wind from high in a tree. It's turning slowly, falling gently from the clouds toward the pond. In the pond, another leaf, a mirror leaf, is rising slowly from the bottom, moving toward the surface. The two leaves move together, meeting exactly where the water meets the air. They come gently together and at that spot, a small wave ripples out and moves toward the edges of the pond. There, in the shallow water at the edges, the wave embraces the grass, which dances its delight.

EXERCISE 2: PROBES ON PARTNERSHIP

After Exercise 1, the mindfulness fantasy, people can stop here, come out of it slowly, and talk about what kind of experience mindfulness is. Or, preferably, they can just go into this next exercise, which consists of probes about partnership. The facilitator simply adds the following:

So, please, let these images fade away and clear a space in your mind. If it's okay with you, I'll make a statement while you are in this open space. Please just let my words in and simply notice what experience is evoked in you by them. It could be feelings or thoughts or both at once. It could be sensations or changes in tension in your body. It could be memories that are evoked, or a change in breathing. If nothing happens, that's okay too. Please just allow my words to speak to you and notice what experiences are evoked by them.

After about two seconds, give the following probe:

Please notice what happens when I tell you . . . We can be partners.

The probe can be repeated after about twenty seconds. People are then invited to discuss in pairs or threes just exactly what they experienced with the probe. The facilitator should encourage people to talk first about the experience they had, the sensations, feelings, thoughts they had, and then elaborate with their associations.

After re-forming into a large group and discussing these experiences, the group re-forms into pairs, with partners taking turns giving this probe and a few others to each other. Other probes might be:

1. *Please notice what happens when I tell you . . . We can be equals.*
2. *Please notice what happens when I tell you . . . We can share the power.*
3. *Please notice what happens when I tell you . . . I won't try to control you.*
4. *Please notice what happens when I tell you . . . I don't want you to control me.*
5. *Please notice what happens when I tell you . . . We are as brother and sister.*

EXERCISE 3: EMBODYING PARTNERSHIP

Part 1: Standing in pairs, guided by the facilitator(s), each person goes inside, eyes closed, and one at a time, takes on these three modes of being: (1) equal with others, (2) dominant, (3) victim. (The facilitator says, for example, *Imagine that you are . . . equal with others.*)

In each case, the facilitator then guides the participants through noticing posture, breathing, energy flow, comfort or tension, feelings, attitudes, and especially how the body is *being used* by the mode of being.

After each mode has been experienced and studied, participants discuss their experiences with partners. The facilitator waits till discussions seem complete, then asks for questions. After questions, a second part of the exercise begins.

Part 2: In fours (or threes), all people start in neutral (for them). All but one person close their eyes and get mindful. While they have their eyes closed, the remaining person goes into one of the modes of being—equal, dominant, or victim. Others, when ready, open their eyes for a second or so, look at the person doing the mode, and study their automatic reactions to that person. When all are ready, the four discuss their experiences. Repeat the process with different people taking on different modes while the others study how they automatically react. In these studies and discussions, we can discover some of our basic ways of dealing with the issues of partnership (equals) and dominance. Large group discussion can follow, stimulated by these experiences.

The Sensitivity Cycle

contributed by Ron Kurtz
Ashland, Oregon

Sensitizing ourselves to ourselves and to others involves going through a cycle something like the following:

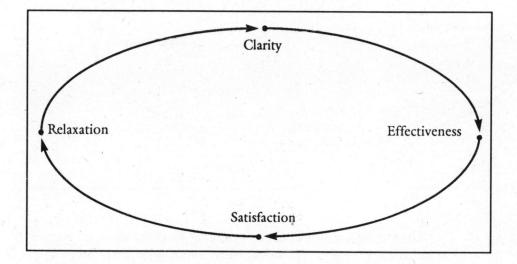

We relax, seeking clarity, effectiveness, and satisfaction.

But along the way are certain barriers we must work through—barriers to insight, response, nourishment, and completion.

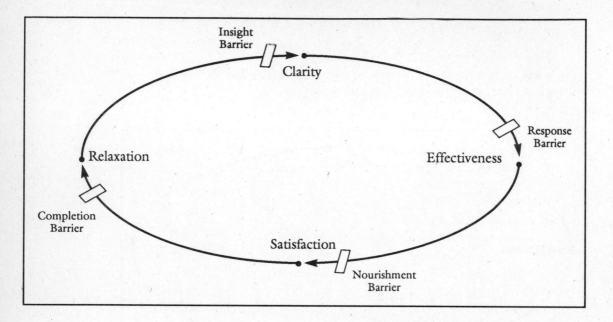

The message of this diagram is that we don't get there all at once. We get there in stages, cycling through these functions and barriers maybe several times before getting where we want to go.

This kind of sensitizing is a vital step in the transition from dominator to partnership living.

The Mondragon Model

contributed by Harry Morel
The Blackforest Mushroom Company
Encinitas, California

I have heard Riane Eisler mention that we need to learn partnership technology and partnership economics. I have been striving toward that goal for many years and think the natural agricultural system is a special window into partnership technology and economics.

To realize the significance of this relationship, we must remember that civilization is still based on agriculture. For this reason, practicing natural agriculture might further partnership economic thinking.

The idea behind this natural agriculture process, developed by Japanese plant pathologist Masanobu Fukuoka, is to let plants grow without too much restriction, to work in partnership with Mother Nature. Some plants are cut down and others are promoted. The soil is not cut and torn up by plowing, thus avoiding erosion. The top layer of the soil, together with the shredded dead biomass that is returned to the earth, provides the fertilizer and the "placenta" for new growth. Insecticides and fungicides are substituted with knowledge of natural insect and disease cycles.

The Mondragon Cooperatives in the Basque region of Spain, which thirty years ago established the country's fastest-growing bank, the Working People's Bank, have developed a blueprint for a very successful partnership business model that could provide the organizational structure for natural agriculture. In "The Mondragon Experiment," a forty-five-minute BBC documentary about this venture, a professor from the London School of Economics shows a hundred percent higher investment efficiency by these worker-owned cooperatives compared with similar corporations. He cites workers living close to their workplace and the trust between management and labor as key factors in the cooperatives' phenomenal productivity.

According to Terry Molner, a partnership business consultant who studied the Mondragon Cooperatives firsthand, a chain of command structure, as seen in stock-holding corporations, is voted into power within a consensus organization in which all members are stockholders and have equal political power. The command structure provides an efficient, coordinated division of labor, yet does not control the organization. The key to this circumstance is that nonworkers are

155

prohibited from owning stock in the company. Since only people who work in the company can own stocks, the command structure remains under the control of the people who are under its control. The circle is complete.

At the general meeting the stockholders set company policy. The directors in the chain of command put this policy into action. The chain of command is a ranked structure in which higher ranks command lower ranks. The command structure itself, however, is organized as a partnership structure in which members are equal in their decision-making and voting power.

In the Mondragon Model, the organizational structure is both pyramidal (ranking) and circular (linking). The top and bottom are connected to form a circular path of power. Ranking serves to identify and utilize people's best talents and capabilities, while linking guarantees freedom and democratic process.

Sexism and War:
Some Useful References

contributed by Dorothy May Emerson
Unitarian Universalist Peace Network
Philadelphia, Pennsylvania

These are a few books we have found useful in working toward the development of a curriculum on what sexism has to do with war. We are most interested in hearing from you concerning your use of these and other related resources. Please write to Dorothy May Emerson, 114 Waverley St., Belmont, MA 02178.

Eisler, Riane. *The Chalice and the Blade*. Harper & Row, 1987.

Geoseffi, Daniella. *Women and War*. McGraw-Hill, 1988.

Gerzon, Mark. *A Choice of Heroes: The Changing Faces of American Manhood*. Houghton Mifflin, 1982.

Gray, Elizabeth Dodson. *Patriarchy as a Conceptual Trap*. Roundtable Press, 1982.

Koen, Susan, and Swaim, Nina. *Ain't Nowhere You Can Run: Handbook for Women on the Nuclear Mentality*. WAND, 1980.

Kopeli, Bruce, and Lakey, George. *Off Their Backs . . . and On Our Own Feet*. New Society Publishers, 1983.

McAllister, Pam, ed. *Reweaving the Web of Life: Feminism and Nonviolence*. New Society Publishers, 1982.

Miller, Jean Baker. *Toward a New Psychology of Women*, 2nd ed. Beacon Press, 1986.

Reardon, Betty. *Sexism and the War System*. Teachers College Press, 1985.

Ruether, Rosemary Radford. "Feminism and Peace." In *Christian Century*, August 31–September 7, 1983.

Sexism and Peacemaking: A Five-Week Curriculum. Unitarian Universalist Peace Network, 5808 Greene St., Philadelphia, PA 19144, (215) 843-2890, 1989.

Strange, Penny. *It'll Make a Man of You . . . A Feminist View of the Arms Race.* Mushroom Books, 10 Heathcote Street, Nottingham, England, 1983.

Women's Encampment for a Future of Peace and Justice Handbook. Women's Peace Camp, 5440 Route 96, Romulus, NY 14541, 1983.

Developing Partnership Skills:
An Invitation to the Reader

contributed by Jennifer S. Macleod, Ph.D.
Princeton Junction, New Jersey

An essential step in the shift to a partnership mode is to develop partnership skills to substitute for the old dominator skills. This is not easy, because we have so little to draw on. Most of our games, customs, institutions, languages, and rituals are structured (whether consciously or unconsciously) to maintain the dominator mode of relating to other human beings and to the earth and its other forms of life.

But there is also a growing body of resources. The issue of how to develop partnership skills has, in one form or another and under a number of different terminologies and with a number of different focuses, been the subject of a number of books. And as we move ahead over the next years and decades, we can optimistically hope for dozens and then hundreds of books and other types of communication, in all languages and in all countries, on the subject.

Perhaps even more important than the communications will be the experiments, the applications in education, in organizations, in negotiations, in local, national, and international efforts.

In the spirit of partnership, we earnestly invite you, the reader, to collaborate with us in gathering and developing a wide variety of ideas, resources, methods, techniques, skills, and materials: ways of developing in ourselves and others the skills we need to function and achieve creatively and effectively in partnership instead of dominator ways. For this particular effort of the Center for Partnership Studies, please send your ideas and suggestions to:

Jennifer S. Macleod, Ph.D.
4 Canoe Brook Drive
Princeton Junction, NJ 08550
Telephone (609) 799-0378

SOME INITIAL THOUGHTS AND IDEAS

Since the subject and the challenge are so vast, this essay can only touch on some of the directions that may be taken, some of the ideas that may be useful.

For example, one might focus on ways of

- eliminating dominator-style "victor vs. vanquished" *competition* in situations in which there is no real conflict, utilizing *collaboration* instead;
- achieving win-win results in conflict situations, so that *both* parties achieve the main substance of what they want; and
- creating and sustaining effective and successful *organizations* that are structured on collaborative, partnership models instead of on power hierarchies in which those in high positions dominate and force the compliance of those in lower positions.

Following is a brief discussion of each of these areas.

CREATING, ACHIEVING, AND SUCCEEDING WITHOUT DOMINATOR-TYPE "WIN-LOSE" COMPETITION

In a dominator society, it is generally assumed that we must create strong competition among individuals and groups in order to motivate them to perform well and achieve difficult goals. In schools, students are pitted one against the other (individually or in groups or teams) in the classroom and on the playing fields. From second grade spelling bees to school athletics and "grading on the curve," to professional sports, to getting promoted on the job, to wars between nations, we are taught that we can only truly win if someone else loses. The race goes to the swift, and everyone else "fails."

There is, however, increasing evidence that fostering such competition does not necessarily improve performance or creativity or achievement, and in fact that it tends to have negative effects instead. This topic has been explored in depth by Alfie Kohn in his book *No Contest: The Case Against Competition* (Houghton Mifflin, 1987), and discussed more briefly in his article of the same name in *New Age Journal* (September/October 1986), and his article "How to Succeed Without Even Vying" in *Psychology Today* (September 1986).

When we begin to think about it, we can see many ways to promote creativity, excellence, and achievement without ever invoking the supposed motivation of beating out someone else. There have always been fine artists and performing artists, creative writers, thinkers, and scientists who have accomplished extraordinary things—individually or with others—without competitiveness ever rearing its head.

In fact, when we think about it, it may become clear that the truly greatest accomplishments have always been those in which beating competitors is not a motivating factor.

Thus, we could profitably examine just about every aspect of our society to see how we can reduce unnecessary competition—the competition that we have artificially created in order to goad people who would otherwise (we thought) perform poorly and achieve little.

The best strategies for reducing competition will probably not be to try to prohibit or campaign against practices such as spelling bees, educational methods that pit student against student, highly competitive "winning is everything" sports such as Little League baseball and professional football, and so forth. Such strategies are likely to meet with very strong opposition, not only because competitive practices seem natural and inevitable in the current dominator-oriented societal structure, but also because people do not see any satisfactory alternatives.

Instead, better strategies may involve the introduction or promotion and encouragement of well-designed partnership-style activities— games, educational methods, athletics, projects of a variety of kinds— that call for and develop skill in collaboration and cooperation. As these grow and show their value, they will provide attractive alternatives that people will begin to turn to by choice.

At some point, dog-eat-dog competitive activities will be seen to be undesirable, and people will be more willing to give them up because there will be better alternatives clearly visible and already proven effective.

Here, for example, is an experiential exercise that could be used in a workshop setting with a group of from four to about ten people.

THE "MAKING MUSIC" EXERCISE
(originated by Jennifer S. Macleod)

Each member of the group is arbitrarily assigned a different simple musical instrument such as an ocarina, a toy piano, a tin flute, a set of drums, a kazoo. If at all possible, each participant should have a different instrument. While they may be toys, the instruments should nevertheless be capable of producing music in tune.

The assignment is a competition to determine which member of the group can produce the best musical performance. Competitiveness is encouraged by the promise of first, second, and third prizes and a congratulatory ceremony. Participants are given about forty-five minutes on their own (they can scatter to different rooms for this) to become familiar with their instruments (without any instruction) and to prepare their performances.

Then, each participant performs for the group, and is graded by the trainer on the quality of the music he or she produces, without regard to any other considerations such as effort, difficulty of the particular instrument, or whatever. The prizes are handed out in a ceremony, with the trainer giving warm praise and congratulations to the winners for being "the best."

Then after a break or lunch, the instruments are reassigned, so that each participant is given a different instrument. This time, the assignment is for the group to produce a musical performance of one or more pieces. The new aim is a cooperative one: to produce the best music possible, with no element of competition. There are no prizes, just the potential satisfaction of achievement. (If feasible, the performance will be tape-recorded and copies made for each participant to take home.)

Again, forty-five minutes is the time allowed. Participants may not switch instruments, but otherwise they are free to organize the effort in any way they see fit. They may if they wish all stay together, or they may break up into smaller groups to prepare separate musical pieces.

The performance should be recorded on audiotape and played back immediately afterward, so that the performers can hear again the music they produced. Then the group discusses and compares the two experiences, their feelings about the exercise and about each other, and the nature and quality of the music produced.

A variation of this exercise would involve arbitrarily separating the participants into two groups, each group being given one of the two assignments described above. The two performances (including the award ceremony for the first group) would be videotaped (or at least audiotaped) and replayed to the total group, brought back together in one room.

The discussion that follows would comprise a full sharing of feelings and observations about the two different experiences and the performances that resulted.

The expectation, of course, is that the collaborative second assignment will not only be a far more effective and enjoyable learning experience, promoting understanding and appreciation as well as musical skill among the participants, but will also result in an obviously better quality of musical performance.

An exercise like this one would not have to be limited to an artistic effort such as music making. For example, a similar design could be used in which the assignment is to solve puzzles, such as the familiar puzzles in which the goal is to separate two or more entangled pieces of twisted rigid metal tubing.

For one group of participants, each could be given a different puzzle, and a competition set up, with first, second, and third prizes to be given to those who solve their puzzles the fastest. For the other group of participants, the assignment would be to see how fast they can—as a group, working together cooperatively—get all the puzzles solved, with no prize but the fun and satisfaction of achievement.

The discussion that followed the experience would, as with the music exercise, compare the experience of each assignment—and the quality of the work accomplished. In all probability, the collaborative approach would result in more of the puzzles being solved more quickly, more learning of what strategies are most effective in solving puzzles of this type, and better communications and relationships among those involved.

ACHIEVING WIN-WIN RESULTS IN CONFLICT SITUATIONS

One of the underlying assumptions in a dominator society is that when two parties (individuals or groups) are in conflict with one another, the only possible outcomes are

- a continuation of the conflict, so that neither party has what it wants (a lose-lose situation),
- a resolution in which one side prevails and gets what it wants, while the other side fails (a win-lose resolution), or
- a compromise, in which each side gets only some of what it wants (this could be termed a lose-lose resolution, even though the two "lose" situations may be some improvement over the earlier situation).

163

There is, however, a fourth possible outcome: a win-win resolution, in which *both* sides achieve the major elements of what they seek. This is a creative solution, often something that neither side even conceived of until they worked together on the challenge of finding such a solution and thus satisfying the needs of both. This type of solution is obviously by far the best possible outcome, yet we, brought up in a dominator society, are often ill-equipped to even conceive that such a solution is possible.

This point can be well illustrated by the following experiential exercise, that might appropriately be called the "How to Win" exercise.

THE "HOW TO WIN" EXERCISE

(Note: The originator of this exercise is unknown to us, but is to be congratulated and thanked, whoever he or she is.)

This exercise is very effective with groups of people; it takes as little as fifteen minutes, and requires no special equipment.

Participants are asked to pair off. (If there is an odd number of participants, the facilitator can participate as a member of a pair, acting in a passive way so as not to "give away" the game.)

The pairs are lined up so that each member of a pair faces the other member, on opposite sides of some line on the floor (such as the edge of a rug or a particular board; or a piece of string can be laid on the floor from one wall to another).

The instructions are that each pair is going to play a game in which the object is to win by getting the other person to cross the line *without speaking or touching*.

Participants are given a minute to decide on their strategy, and then the game begins. Participants are instructed that as soon as there is a "win" in their particular pair, they are to continue no further, but should sit down quietly and watch other pairs without comment.

Depending upon the time available and what is happening with the pairs, the facilitator either lets every pair reach some conclusion (or give up totally), or calls a halt after the first one or two pairs sit down.

What usually happens is that there is much gesticulating, mock inviting or threatening behavior, offers of dollar bills, laughter, signs of exasperation, and so forth. Sometimes one member of the pair "gives up" and crosses the line to the other side, at which point there may be triumphant celebration by the "victor" or friendly conciliatory hugging.

Sooner or later, the members of at least one pair will step across the line.

Typically, pairs in whom there was no resolution—no one crossed the line—are frustrated and puzzled, and perhaps irritated with one another.

Pairs in which *one* person crossed the line may be reconciled, because the "vanquished" is treated well by the "victor." However, the "loser" is also left puzzled, frustrated, and defeated because he or she is aware of a failure to figure out the game and win.

Pairs in which both individuals cross the line simultaneously typically react in one of two ways:

- One or both members of the pair are left feeling frustrated or puzzled, because they think that really they *both* lost.
- Or if they both "won," the win was not a "real" win because the other one did not *lose*.

In the debriefing discussion that follows, the leader helps participants to see that in our society, we are taught that for every winner there must be a loser—while, in fact, that is neither necessary nor desirable. The aim in every conflict situation should be to find a solution that pleases *both* sides—and the best way to do that involves cooperation between the parties.

The reader who would like to explore the concepts and strategies of negotiation (conflict resolution) that creates solutions or agreements that meet the most important needs and desires of both parties may want to read Roger Fisher and William Ury, *Getting to Yes: Negotiating Agreement Without Giving In* (hardcover Houghton Mifflin, 1981; softcover Penguin Books, 1983) and Roger Fisher and Scott Brown's more recent *Getting Together: Building Relationships* (Houghton Mifflin, 1988).

CREATING AND SUSTAINING EFFECTIVE, SUCCESSFUL ORGANIZATIONS AND INSTITUTIONS WITHOUT DOMINATOR HIERARCHIES

We are all very familiar with hierarchical institutions and organizations, from the family to the largest corporations and governments; and the hierarchies are based on domination by those with power over the others. In the dominator model, this is inevitable.

But if we are to develop societies and cultures on the partnership model, we will have to (and will want to) have institutions and organizations that are modeled not on dominator hierarchies, but on cooperation and collaboration instead.

This is a very tall order. While we may be able to see ways to decrease destructive competition, and to conduct negotiations in win-win ways, we may currently know and understand far less about how to create organizations/institutions on the partnership model. For doesn't the elimination of the dominator hierarchy mean anarchy, chaos, and an organization that has no structure—and no effectiveness—whatever?

In fact, there are some important signposts to other ways. Non-hierarchical (not based on a dominator hierarchy) does not mean structureless. Nor does it mean that everyone has to be paid the same or do the same thing, nor that all tasks—including managing—are rotated among everyone.

What it *can* mean is that all individuals in an organization are there by choice, and take part in decisions as to what role they play, how they work together, and how the work and the organization are structured. The glue that binds the organization together is in fact the common goal, which each individual freely chooses to make one of her or his personal goals as well. Leaders may (and usually will) exist, but they are leaders who emerge by virtue of their expertise and, particularly, their ability to inspire and help others to work well together for common goals.

Within the discipline of supervisory and management training, many experiential exercises have been found useful in helping people understand and develop skills in organizing and working in collaborative ways without the power hierarchies of bosses and subordinates.

For example, workshop participants can be given materials such as foam board, rulers and T-squares, cutting equipment, glue and tape, and be given the assignment of building something such as a model house within a tight time schedule. They then organize themselves for the task along whatever lines they choose.

If such an exercise is videotaped, participants learn a great deal about what works well and what doesn't work well in cooperative projects. If the same group is then given another (different) assignment, they usually work better the second time, differentiating roles and cooperating and sharing more effectively, and producing a better result more efficiently.

There are many variations on such exercises. For example, one group may be given the assignment with the structure left to their own devising, while another group has hierarchical roles arbitrarily assigned, with a requirement that they work in that structure. The two groups then compare their experience and results. Or the same group may be given one assignment without an assigned hierarchy, and one with, so that participants can directly compare their own experiences in each structure.

Small group cooperation in workshops is, of course, a far cry from effective partnership structures for bigger ongoing organizations. It remains exceedingly difficult for organizations, even if they started along partnership lines, to sustain such patterns when surrounded by a larger society and culture that is determinedly and oppressively "dominator" in style.

Reason for optimism exists, however. As people make the effort, and as some succeed in creating and sustaining small and then larger organizations on the partnership model, their success and high performance and achievement will begin to be noticed, and others will become interested in trying the new approaches.

For example, William L. Gore, in his article "The Lattice Organization: A Philosophy of Enterprise" (*Networking Journal,* Spring/Summer 1985), describes an organizational structure based on the lattice, in which each person interacts directly with every other person with no intermediary. There is only "natural" leadership—no assigned or assumed authority. This, he says, can be an extremely effective structure in organizations small enough so that everyone knows everyone else.

In organizations larger than that, the challenge is greater—but not impossible to meet. For example, Charles F. Kiefer and Peter M. Senge, in their monograph *Metanoic Organizations: Experiments in Organizational Innovation* (Innovation Associates Inc., 1982), describe and discuss an approach to larger-scale organizational structure that is clearly in line with the partnership model.

They call such organizations "metanoic," from the Greek word *metanoia,* meaning a fundamental shift of mind (*meta,* transcending;

noia, mind). These organizations are based upon the development of a powerful vision and purpose—something that everyone in or attracted to the organization is inspired by and becomes aligned with, so that all involved take full shared responsibility for the success of the whole. In such an organization, there can be tremendous flexibility and creativity in structure, roles, functions—and results far beyond usual expectations.

This approach, say Kiefer and Senge, has brought striking success to a number of actual companies. The Basque cooperatives in Spain, for example, have much to show us. (See "The Mondragon Model" earlier in this section.) These and other groups, such as the Baha'i and the Quakers, have created structures that have required them to develop partnership skills, and we can learn from these pioneers in partnership development and practical application.

MOVING TOWARD PARTNERSHIP

This has been only a brief discussion of some of the possible approaches to developing partnership skills. However, it points toward the vast and exciting challenges of moving as quickly and effectively as we can to provide attractive alternatives to the doleful and destructive dominator behavior that has shaped human society for the past five thousand years.

As mentioned earlier, I hope that you, the reader, will have ideas to contribute to this effort, and will send them to me at the address given earlier.

Re-Membering, Re-Evaluating, Re-Leasing, and Re-Entering

contributed by Karen-Elise Clay
Chicago, Illinois

RE-MEMBERING OUR CHILDHOOD– THE SELF AND THE EARTH

DISCUSSION

(Allow approximately thirty minutes for this exercise.)

Childhood is a time of vulnerability, learning, and growth. Each of us learned different things from our parents and society connected with our gender.

Break into small groups and discuss any or all of the following questions.

1. What did you feel about being raised a female/male?
2. What limitations were placed on you because you were female/male?
3. What was your experience with the educational system?
4. What messages did you receive about your femaleness or maleness from your religion?
5. What adult models did you have?
6. What was your experience in the home—mother, other siblings?
7. Did you limit yourself because of your sex?

After twenty minutes, come together in a large group and ask each small group to share some of the highlights from the experience.

RE-EVALUATING OUR FEMALE/MALE RELATIONSHIPS

DISCUSSION AND ROLE PLAYS

(Allow approximately twenty-five minutes for this exercise.)

Break into small groups of three or four and discuss times when you experienced successful partnership in your own life.

For example, you may have shared in Lamaze childbirth. Keep in mind that partnership may occur between man and man, or man and woman, or woman and woman, or between an individual and an organization, to name just a few possible combinations.

Taking an example from your discussion, create a role play to share with the group.

RE-LEASING FEMALE AND MALE POWER

STORYWRITING

(Allow approximately twenty-five minutes for this exercise.)

Ask people to form groups of three to six people. Ask them to choose an option from the following:

1. Write a story from the perspective of the partnership model depicting one of the following topics:

   rearing children
   marriage
   education
   the workplace

2. Rewrite a well-known story (from a movie, book, fairy tale, etc.) relating it from the perspective of the partnership model.

After the groups have finished, ask each of the groups to briefly share the story.

RE-ENTERING: MOVING TOWARD PERSONAL AND PLANETARY ACTION

ROLE PLAY

(Allow approximately thirty minutes for this exercise.)

Break into groups of two to four and create a role play using the partnership model to respond to one of the following situations, or create your own situation.

1. Your teenage daughter comes home an hour after curfew, a curfew to which you had mutually agreed. You . . .
2. Your husband, who is the sole support of the family, comes home tired and distraught. He tells you he cannot continue at his present job. You . . .
3. The teacher of your ten-year-old son calls you to say your son has not been completing his homework and is a frequent disruption in the class. You . . .
4. As the mother of a young child you feel resentment building toward your husband for not contributing more to help with housework and child care. You . . .
5. Your roommate continually leaves "messes" in the kitchen area, even after you have requested her respect for mutual living space. You . . .

CLOSING

To close this session, the facilitator reads aloud: "In this moment we are joined to share thoughts, feelings, and hopes for the future, individually and together. Let us weave tomorrow from our dreams of love and wisdom in partnership with all of life on Earth."

Ideas for Workshops and More Discussion Topics and Exercises

contributed by Marsha Utain and Arthur Melville
Long Beach, California

These are ideas for discussions, exercises, and workshops in a number of areas involved in dominator to partnership shifts in our lives.

They are based on these readings: *The Chalice and the Blade* by Riane Eisler; *Bradshaw on the Family* by John Bradshaw (chapters 1–3); "The Drama Triangle and the Emotion Diamond" in *Stepping Out of Chaos* by Marsha Utain; and *Scream Louder* by Marsha Utain and Barbara Oliver.

An easy way to get started is to ask participants to share what in the readings has been most important or meaningful and most distressing or difficult for them.

DISCUSSION TOPICS

1. To focus on family structure and its influence on our lives:
   - List various ways the hierarchical family structure feeds and is part of the dominator model.
   - List various covert and overt family rules that set the context for you to be a part of the dominator model.
   - Rewrite the family rules. Now imagine yourself as both the child you were and the adult you are. Write a letter to your inner child telling the child that it is no longer necessary for the child to obey the old rules. Also imagine the child in front of you and talk to the child. Let the child write back to you or talk with you.
   - Do some emotional healing work with the inner child. Spend time listening to the inner child tell you how difficult it was growing up in a dominator-model family.

2. We need to distinguish between spirituality and religion. Most of us were raised in our families in dominator models of religion. To discover and change those models:

   - Write down a list of your religious beliefs.
   - Write down who taught them to you, when, and how.
   - Notice if fear was involved in the teaching process.
   - Notice if fear or compulsion or rigidity or retribution is involved in the practice of religion.
   - Take your list, place it on a chair opposite you, imagine the people in your life who gave you your beliefs, and give them back their beliefs.
   - Start a new list and place on it what you want and need from a Higher Power and a religion.
   - Use beliefs that are nurturing and supportive.
   - Recognize your Higher Power as a Being of love, support, creativity, generosity, nurturance, guidance, rather than punishment, destruction.
   - Remember a time when you were very small and felt close to nature.
   - Write a fairy tale or story about a child and nature with a loving, supportive environment.
   - Spend time in nature. Be aware of the life within the plants and animals around you.

3. To operate in a healthy partnership way, communications, both personal and societal, must be direct, clear, and honest. To focus on communications:

   - Write out clear, honest, direct communications to the people in your life with whom you feel incomplete. Practice in your partnership group or with a safe friend. Then send the communications to the people for whom they were originally intended. Notice if you are afraid to do this with any one person. If so, you may be dealing with a person who knows only the dominator model.
   - Tell someone about a need you have that is unmet. Get support for achieving it.
   - Expose rules of secrecy in your family in a safe environment.
   - Discover and list the secrets in your family of origin. If

you are comfortable with this, share them with friends in a safe environment.

- Discover and list the rules that kept the secrets. Write down who created the rules and how the rules protected them.

4. Many of our individual problems relate back to our inability to recognize and deal with our emotions. The dominator model of society perceives the emotions as effeminate and unacceptable. Dominator-model families ignore, squelch, ridicule, and deny emotions. Yet, no matter how cognitive we may believe we are, we are frequently run by the emotions we refuse to acknowledge. After learning about the Emotion Diamond, write down some instances or events in your life that are unresolved.

- Find the emotions that you are feeling in or about the circumstances.
- Be willing to experience the emotions.
- Communicate your emotions to the people involved. If you do not feel safe, write them a letter that you do not send. Keep writing letters until you feel the emotion subsiding. Get some support for resolving the issues.

5. Agreements that mutually support people are important in a partnership world. Making agreements is necessary when we have different needs and desires.

- Learn how to make agreements and understand the need for agreements in a partnership world. Agreements are specific. The terms are well defined; they are acceptable to all parties involved. Failure to meet the terms of the agreement is dealt with as part of the agreement.
- Learn how to renegotiate agreements. Recognize that you must do that prior to the end of the term of the agreement.

6. Personal obstacles include fear of being wrong about your life and beliefs, fear of letting go, fear of the unknown, fear of your emotions, fear of others' emotions, fear of others' judgments, fear of harm, and not having adequate tools to deal with the obstacles. Some tools for dealing with obstacles:

- Make a list of all the things you are afraid to be wrong about. Imagine the consequences of being wrong. Who else is involved? Are they judging you?

- Write a letter to the people you are afraid are judging you. Tell them how you feel about it and what you want.

- Imagine being the people you have written to and write a letter to yourself from their perspective.

- Imagine the people you have written to in chairs around you. Talk to them and have them talk back.

- Now imagine that their judgments are not accurate and that you will suffer no consequences.

- Redo the exercises from this perspective.

7. To focus on control and manipulation versus personal power, and to help us let go:

- Think of all the people and things in life that you have tried to manipulate and control.

- List the honest reasons for this. Tell what you have been afraid of.

- Write a list of things that you need and want. Ask people around you to help you find honest, assertive ways to get what you want and need.

- Write down all the things you have denied and been dishonest about concerning yourself and your family and any other structures that you have belonged to, such as information, problems about the past, and motivations.

- Write out the beliefs about and worse fears that come up when you face each item on your "afraid-to-be-wrong about" list. Where did the fears come from?

8. How do men move from the present archetypes of the dominator model to new archetypes of the partnership model? (See "Getting Started" in Session 4.)

- Write a new story with partnership male archetypes. Share it with people of both sexes. Get honest feedback about what the archetype promote.

- Write new fairy tales for children using the partnership male models and archetypes. Share them with people

175

of both sexes. Get honest feedback about what the models and archetype promote.

- Write poetry for all age groups using the partnership male models and archetypes. Share it with people of both sexes. Get honest feedback about what the models and archetype promote.
- Create artwork for all the above.

9. How do women move from the present archetypes of the dominator model to the new archetypes of the partnership model? (See "Getting Started" in Session 4.)

- Write a new story with partnership female archetypes. Share it with people of both sexes. Get honest feedback about what the archetype promotes.
- Write new fairy tales for children using the partnership female models. Share them with people of both sexes. Get honest feedback about what the model and archetype promote.
- Write poetry for all age groups using the partnership female models and archetypes. Share it with people of both sexes. Get honest feedback about what the models and archetype promote.
- Create artwork for all the above.

PARTNERSHIP
RESOURCES

Love, joy, and the grace, beauty and wonder of life is captured in these ancient partners—two birds from the famous Spring Fresco with its extravagant vegetation uncovered in the excavation of the Minoan settlement on the island of Thera near Crete. They were painted about 1500 B.C. Line drawing from the original: Jim Beeman.

The Partnership and the Dominator Models: Basic Configurations

The table and diagrams that follow give a bird's-eye view of the three key components of the partnership and dominator models. They are useful as a quick introduction to systems thinking about society.

A COMPARISON OF THE THREE BASIC COMPONENTS OF THE DOMINATOR AND THE PARTNERSHIP MODELS

COMPONENT	DOMINATOR MODEL	PARTNERSHIP MODEL
Gender Relations	The ranking of the male over the female, as well as the higher valuing of the traits and social values stereotypically associated with "masculinity" rather than "femininity"[1]	Equal valuing of the sexes as well as of "femininity" and "masculinity," or a sexually equalitarian social and ideological structure
Violence	A high degree of institutionalized social violence, including wife beating, rape, and warfare, with violence a structural component of the system	A low degree of social violence, with violence, including wife beating, rape, and warfare, not a structural component of the system
Social Structure	A generally hierarchic[2] and authoritarian social organization, with the degree of authoritarianism and hierarchism roughly corresponding to the degree of male dominance	A generally equalitarian social structure

1. As used here, *masculinity* and *femininity* refer to the dominator stereotypes that associate "real" men with aggression, heroic violence, lack of feeling, and other "hard" traits, and only women with "soft" traits like caring, nonviolence, and compassion. Clearly, there are many caring and compassionate men; and women, as well as men, are capable of violent and uncaring behavior. We want to stress this important distinction, as well as the point that in a partnership model of society, *femininity* and *masculinity* would have different meanings.

2. As used here, the term *hierarchic* refers to what we may call a *domination* hierarchy, or the type of hierarchy inherent in a dominator model of social organization, based on force or the threat of force. Such hierarchies should be distinguished from a second type of hierarchy, which for clarity can be called an *actualization* hierarchy—for example, of molecules, cells, and organs in the body: a progression toward a higher and more complex level of functioning.

The following diagrams indicate how the relationships between the three major components of the two models are interactive, with all three mutually reinforcing one another.

Dominator Model:

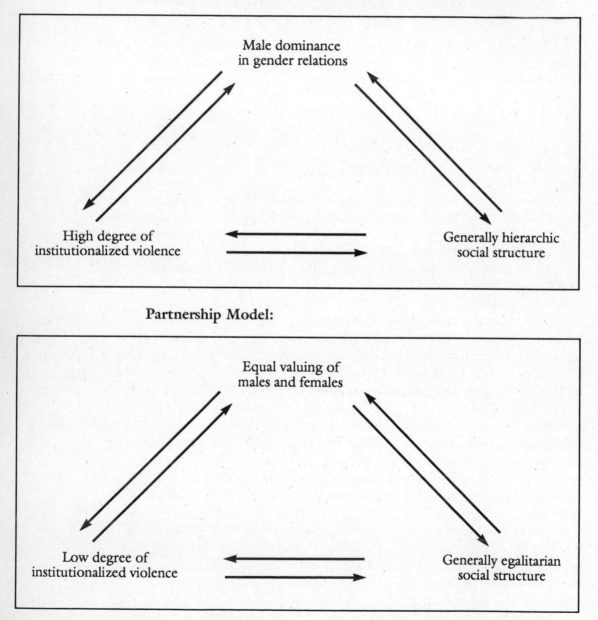

Partnership Model:

The Partnership and Dominator Models

*How to recognize them when you see them
and move toward a less tense, more fulfilling life*

Many of us are trying to change patterns that cause us pain and hold back our personal and social development. To do this, we are trying to identify what we want to hang on to and what we want to leave behind. It is a question, so to speak, of not throwing out the baby with the bath water. Where and how do we draw the line?

This is where the partnership and dominator models can be such effective tools for the liberation of our minds. When we use these models to identify what is going on in every area of our lives, we begin to say to ourselves things like, "That is a dominator belief, attitude, behavior, or process—and I want no more of it," or "This is a partnership belief, attitude, behavior, or process—and this is the way I want to be." By developing and using these basic tools—and this basic way of thinking about everything in our lives—we create key building blocks for the partnership future.

The two tables that follow show some of the main differences between the partnership and dominator models. The first table presents some of the differences between the partnership and dominator models that can be summarized in a single word or phrase. The second table explores some of the more complex and subtle differences.

While differentiation is one of our most important thinking and learning tools, it is important to keep in mind that sometimes the differences between how these two models are manifested in actual practice is a question of degree or emphasis. And some of the contrasts that may initially come to mind, such as the idea that cooperation is only a partnership trait and competition is found only in dominator systems, are too simplistic—and thus not helpful.

There *is* cooperation in the dominator model. A notable example is the cooperation of groups of men to conquer and/or suppress others, be they a modern army or the inquisitors of the Middle Ages. But as the second table indicates, it is a cooperation founded on fear and aggression toward an "out-group."

Similarly, there *is* competition in the partnership model. But in contrast to competition in the dominator model, it is not the exploitive "dog-eat-dog" competition where our natural human capacity for empathy has been insensitized by dominator socialization (as has particularly been the case in the upbringing of men). It is a different kind of competition: achievement-oriented rather than winning-oriented, modulated and regulated by feelings of empathy with others rather than by a drive to suppress and conquer others at any cost (as expressed in the well-known adage "all's fair in love and war").

Moreover, while a basic difference between a dominator and a partnership society is that the first is held together primarily by fear and the second by trust, this is not to say that even in a society that approaches very closely the partnership model, we would never be afraid or mistrustful. The difference—and it is major—is that in a dominator society, fear is systematically inculcated in us and trust (beginning with the trust between the female and male halves of humanity) is systematically undermined through dominator cultural myths and social institutions.

This leads to a very important point: the partnership society is *not* a utopian, ideal society free of problems, conflicts, disappointments, or grief. Conflict is a natural aspect of life, as different organisms with different needs, purposes, and plans come together. Grief and disappointment are also inherent in life, if only because we must all die.

The difference—and again it is a major one—lies in how we are taught to deal with these givens. For example, in the dominator model, conflict is emphasized, but at the same time the violent suppression of conflict is institutionalized, and might is equated with right. By contrast, in the partnership model, conflict is openly recognized, and dealing with it creatively in ways where both parties learn and grow is encouraged.

Another important point to stress is that the difference between partnership and dominator beliefs, attitudes, behaviors, and processes is not a matter of "us" versus "them," for as Walt Kelly's Pogo said, "I have met the enemy and he is us." Both models operate within each of us.

In some of us the dominator model runs rampant. In others the partnership model is afraid to emerge except in wholly protected circumstances. In still others the partnership model is already quite strong. But every one of us faces the challenge of creating for ourselves new habits of thinking, feeling, and acting—habits appropriate for a world where we can live more harmoniously with one another and our natural habitat. This is why knowing what the dominator model is, where it came from, how it operates within us and upon us, and what to do about it—and knowing what the partnership model is, where it came from, how it operates within us and upon us, and how to use it—is of central importance in this time of confusion. Recognizing the models is essential for our own clarity and for human advancement.

In all these charts there is room for you to add your ideas. We invite you to send the best of these to us at the Center for Partnership Studies, 51936, Pacific Grove, CA 93950.

KEY WORDS COMPARISON OF THE DOMINATOR AND PARTNERSHIP MODELS

DOMINATOR MODEL	PARTNERSHIP MODEL
fear	trust
win/lose orientation	win/win orientation
power over	power to/with
male dominance	gender partnership
sadomasochism	mutual pleasure
control	nurture
ranking	linking
one-sided benefit	mutual benefit
manipulation	open communication
destruction	actualization
hoarding	sharing
codependency	interdependency
left-brain thinking	whole-brain thinking
negative conditioning	positive conditioning
violence against others	empathy with others
taking orders	working in teams
alienation	integration
nuclear arms race	international partnership
war	peace
secrecy	openness/accountability
coercion	participation
indoctrination	education
conquest of nature	respect for nature
conformity	creativity

KEY CONCEPTS COMPARISON OF THE DOMINATOR
AND PARTNERSHIP MODELS

DOMINATOR MODEL	PARTNERSHIP MODEL
Cooperation based on fear and aggression toward "out-group"	Cooperation based on trust and reciprocity with other groups
Arbitrary freedom for a few	Empathetic freedom for everyone
Those who are different seen as inferior	Celebration of diversity
Women and men seen as opposites in "war of sexes"	Men and women seen as human beings who are different but not inferior or superior
Masculinity[1] equated with domination and femininity with submission	Masculinity and femininity seen as having both active and passive components
"Masculine" values such as conquest and domination given precedence	"Feminine" values such as caring and nonviolence given precedence
High degree of violence, ranging from rape, child abuse, and wife battering to war, modeled through sacred and secular images to maintain force-based rankings	Linking as primary principle of organization manifested in images that celebrate life-giving, life-maintaining, and life-enhancing activities
Male images of heroic violence institutionalized and sanctified	Male images of gentle nurturance honored
Chronic hatred and fear systematically inculcated	Chronic hatred and fear recognized as outcome of an imbalanced social and ideological system; trust (between races, countries, women and men) supported through ideology and institutions
Violence and sexual conquest idealized at the same time that law and order are touted as central to social control	Violence is seen for what it is and mutual respect rather than control are central to concepts of law and order
Femininity portrayed as indirect and manipulative, and devalued	Femininity portrayed as creative and nurturing, and honored.
Inventiveness by a few men supported to maintain the dominator system (as in ever "better" weapons and fear-instilling images and myths)	Creativity by everyone supported to actualize both women's and men's higher individual and social potentials
Woman imaged as idealized virgin/mother or dishonored witch/whore, primarily as relational to a man	Woman imaged as full-fledged human being, neither vilified nor idealized, powerful in her own right, both spiritually and temporally
Leader as a man (and occasional woman) who gives orders to subordinates or followers	Leader as a woman or man who inspires others to work for commonly agreed-on goals

184

Conquest/exploitation-oriented, insensitive competition	Achievement-oriented, empathetic competition
Conflict is emphasized, but at the same time the violent suppression of conflict through "winning" and "conquest" is encouraged—in fact, idealized	Conflict is recognized as natural among different individuals with different needs and desires, but the peaceful resolution of conflict through win/win approaches is encouraged
People treated as means	People treated as ends
Fear and scarcity seen as key motivations for worker productivity	Satisfaction from participation in decision making and sharing in profits and other benefits seen as key motivations for productivity
Manager seen as a controller or cop who gives orders that others follow unquestioningly	Manager seen as one who inspires and encourages participation in production by working teams
Planning is short-term with little thought for future generations	Planning also entails long-term concern for present and future generations
Artificial scarcity is created through war and waste to maintain an exploitive economics and politics of fear	Abundance is jointly created and shared, with the highest value given to the caring work that keeps society going
Quantity of possessions substituted for satisfying human relations	Quality of human relations and material goods emphasized
Domination or power-over becomes an addiction, along with addiction to abusive relationships and harmful substances as means of escaping chronic stress	Mutual support and satisfaction provide a basic sense of self-esteem, leading to interdependency rather than codependency
Selected parts of the social and ecological system focused on, resulting in chronic imbalances in perception and action	Holistic or systems thinking encouraged, resulting in more balanced ways of perceiving the world and living in it
Society seen as a stable machine with people as expendable cogs	Society viewed as an adaptive structure with people as involved cocreators
The Earth imaged as an object to be conquered and exploited	The Earth imaged as a living organism of which we are a part

1. As used here, *masculinity* and *femininity* refer to the dominator stereotypes that associate "real" men with aggression, heroic violence, lack of feeling, and other "hard" traits, and only women with "soft" traits like caring, nonviolence, and compassion. Clearly, there are many caring and compassionate men; and women, as well as men, are capable of violent and uncaring behavior. We want to stress this important distinction, as well as the point that in a partnership model of society, *femininity* and *masculinity* would have different meanings.

Everyday Partnership Action Chart

This chart is a personal tool for partnership action in our everyday lives.* It is designed to serve as a partnership agreement with ourselves, clearly setting forth the changes we want to make in key areas of our lives, such as taking better care of our physical and mental health; relationships with our parents, children, friends, lovers, and/or spouses; our work relations; our community participation; the spiritual or religious dimension of our life; our involvement in politics, education, economics, the arts, the media, and other key areas of society.

It is a chart for you to use to meet your particular needs. We have started it off with a few examples that may or may not be relevant for you. Its main purpose is to help you formulate your own partnership agenda and specific ways for turning it into action.

The examples come from many different areas. You could take any one and develop a much more specific agenda. The main thing we have tried to do here is to emphasize personal involvement and responsibility, the "everydayness" of the partnership way, and the importance of committing to doable action. Like New Year's resolutions, these promises to ourselves must be kept in the realm of the possible. Forming a support group to offer feedback and share progress reports will also help, as we work to make these important changes.

While this is your own private chart, it is also a tool for participatory action research. So please send us your best and most practical action-oriented ideas (those that really work for you) and we will try to share them with others through the Center for Partnership Studies.

*This chart was the creation of Robin Van Doren, and we want to gratefully acknowledge her contribution.

186

THE DOMINATOR WAY	THE PARTNERSHIP WAY	ACTION
The way I did it in the past	The way I want to do it now	Changes to make
Ordered my children around	Explain things to my children and enlist their cooperation	Plan time together with my family to work out shared responsibility
Feared those in positions of authority	Respect authority (in the original Latin sense of the word *auctoritas,* or the source of production and invention) in myself and others	Ask questions when needed Take responsibility for my decisions and actions Say "no" to actions that violate my integrity or the integrity of others Find the "common ground"
Deferred totally to external medical advice	Discover the wisdom of partnering my body	Change to healthier eating patterns Allow time for relaxation Notice changes that occur and modify actions on the basis of these changes
Ignored the environmental impact of what I did	Make myself a responsible partner with the environment	Recycle newspapers, cans, bottles, and other used things Work for legislation that stops or prevents exploitation of environment
Watched TV and movies that depict violence, greed, and exploitation	Watch media that support partnership and caring	Look for programs and movies that support partnership Write to TV channels to support these programs Make lists of good programming available to schools, libraries, and others and share this information Work on local, national, and/or international media to print and broadcast more partnership images, stories, documentaries, and news Create images and stories that support partnership

The early love of music can be seen in this sketch (left) based on a Cycladic flutist sculpted in highly polished white marble found in Keros, near Amorgos. This one dates back to the third century B.C. A harpist carved in white marble (right), also found in Keros, near Amorgos, in the Cyclades Islands, also dates back to the third century B.C. Line drawings from the originals: Jeff Helwig.

The Language of Partnership

In trying to shift from a dominator to a partnership way of thinking and living, a major obstacle is our language. How can we think and live as partners if the words in our heads keep reinforcing dominator stereotypes?

Words have a powerful effect on how we think and act. For example, Eskimos have a number of different words for snow, enabling them to distinguish between various conditions others simply see as one. This is an example of how words shape the way we see the world. The use of words like *boy* to address a grown man in both the American South and many Asian and African colonies is an example of how words serve to define people as inferior, thereby helping to maintain them in a subordinate position. When strangers call grown women "girls" or address them as "dear" or "honey," they are conveying a similarly patronizing message.

The semantics of power relations are particularly striking in the use of words that serve to define the relationship of women and men. In English, for example, the ostensibly generic use of words like *mankind, man,* and *he* to include both sexes unconsciously conditions both women and men to think in male-centered ways, effectively teaching us that women are secondary or do not count. Similarly, words like *chairman* or *congressman* teach us to associate only men with positions of power, effectively discouraging women from aspiring to such positions, except in "exceptional" cases. The use of words like *emasculate* or *effeminate* to express negative meanings further teaches us to value men and "masculinity" over women and anything associated with "femininity."

Today, as the equal value and equal rights of *all* people are increasingly asserted, changes in language are also being recognized as important steps toward the creation of a just society. But these changes are not easy to make. Because linguistic habits are established very early in life, it is difficult to break them. Moreover, languages that are the product of male-dominated societies tend to lack words that express a different world view.

The following terms already in common usage are a few suggestions for those who want to break out of the prison of words that unconsciously force us to think of one half of humanity as less valuable than the other.

DOMINATOR LANGUAGE	PARTNERSHIP LANGUAGE
mankind	humanity/humankind
man	human
he	she or he/one/they
chairman	chairperson/chair
congressman	congressperson
man hours	work hours
man power	work power, work force
to man	to staff
gentlemen	ladies and gentlemen
Dear Sir	Dear Madam and Sir/Dear Sir or Madam/Dear Madam or Sir/Dear Manager
emasculated	weak/nonassertive
effeminate	decadent/weak
statesman	diplomat/leader/policymaker
sissy	sensitive boy
brotherhood	community/kinship/friendship/unity/partnership
craftsman	artisan/skilled worker
spokesman	speaker/spokesperson/representative
common man	average person

Human Rights:
Toward an Integrated Theory for Action

by Riane Eisler

This article has previously appeared in Feminist Issues *(Spring 1987),* Human Rights Quarterly *(August 1987), and* Nordic Journal on Human Rights *(August 5, 1987).*

Introduction

Modern history has been shaped by the struggle for human rights. Though this struggle has been successful in important respects, human rights are still, at best, tenuous. Rather than steadily advancing, we are constantly forced to refight the same battles. Instead of becoming firmly rooted, even gains we have already made are chronically in jeopardy.

This article proceeds from three basic premises bearing on these problems: that the aim of the international human rights movement is to secure protection for individual rights; that this includes the rights of all human beings; and that, without a theory that integrates the human rights of half of humanity, the goal of the human rights movement, equal justice for all, cannot be attained.

The discussion that follows provides a historical overview of both the human rights and women's rights movements, examines some of the consequences of this separation for both women and society at large, and proposes that the construction of a unified action-oriented theory of human rights that may be applied to the *whole* of humanity—women as well as men— is now not only essential but also feasible.

The departure point, and juridical foundation, for such a theory is the gradual recognition by the United Nations of the right of women to the "exercise and enjoyment of human rights and fundamental freedoms on a basis of equality with men,"[1] culminating in the Convention on the Elimination of All Forms of Discrimination Against Women. The Charter of the United Nations affirms the dignity and worth of all persons without distinctions as to race, religion, or sex. A number of subsequent UN declarations and conventions directly or indirectly address violations of the human rights of women.[2] But when, in December 1979, the UN General Assembly adopted this historic Convention, it marked the first time that the right of half of humanity to protection from oppressive practices embedded in laws and customs was forcefully addressed by this important international body.

This action was not only an important step toward the attainment of the three interrelated goals of the First United Nations Decade for Women: Equality, Development, and Peace;[3] it also greatly accelerated the process of ending the principal legal distinctions that have traditionally excluded the rights of women from the purview of human rights activities.

Human Rights and Women's Rights

Human rights have traditionally been defined as "men's inalienable right to life, liberty, and property."[4] The term "men" has sometimes been said to include women. But this has not been reflected in human rights theory or in its application.

Modern theories of "human rights" and "women's rights" have historically developed in two separate theoretical strains. Leading philosophers writing on the "rights of man," such as John Locke in the seventeenth century and Jean Jacques Rousseau in the eighteenth century, specifically articulated a double standard of thought. Men were defined as individuals innately possessed of certain "natural rights." Women, on the other hand, were defined not as individuals but as members of men's households and thus, along with their offspring, under male control.[5] In response, women—such as Mary Wollstonecraft and Abigail Adams in the eighteenth century, Elizabeth Cady Stanton and Sojourner Truth in the nineteenth, and masses of women from both the developing and developed world in the 20th century—pressed for "women's rights." Women, they argued, are also individuals entitled to the same basic rights and freedoms as men.[6]

Nonetheless, the international movement for human rights has focused primarily on the rights of one half of humanity: men. Human rights theories continue to deal primarily with the so-called public or political sphere. Since women traditionally have been excluded from this sphere, this has in effect served to also exclude the rights of women from the category of rights protected from institutionalized oppression and discrimination. Even today, when women have made some inroads into the outside or "man's world," relations between women and men—along with women themselves—are in many nations largely confined to the familial or private sphere. So, in actual practice, international agencies working for the advancement of human rights continue to focus primarily on the relations between men and men.[7]

A traditional rationale for separating the private from the public sphere has been that what a man does in the confines of his home is strictly an internal affair. By contrast, the idea that what governments do within the confines of their nations is a strictly internal affair has today explicitly been rejected by human rights advocates. Indeed, the rejection of this idea is the theoretical basis for the international human rights movement.[8]

The international human rights movement recognizes that terms like "national sovereignty" or "national security" are frequently code words for maintaining a particular regime in power. But the idea that what national governments do should not be the subject of "outside interference" is both historically and conceptually a direct derivative of a far more entrenched idea. This is the traditional tenet that the male head of the family is entitled to rule over "his" women and children without any outside interference with "family autonomy" or "family integrity," terms that are frequently also code words for the preservation of male power. Both these ideas are inherent in patriarchal or androcratic thinking, deriving from the primitive notion that "a man's home is his castle," in other words, his private autocratic domain.

How integrally connected these two ideas have been may be seen in the English common law, which both linguistically and in specific penal provisions equated the "right" of kings to rule nations and the "right" of men to rule households. In the English common law, husband and wife were called *baron* and *feme*. That the word *baron* is to be taken literally, as signifying a ruler, is dramatically illustrated by the fact that if the *feme* killed her *baron* she was not punished as if she had killed another person. The law treated such a killing as a form of treason, and condemned her to the same terrible public punishment by torture as if she had killed the king.[9]

A commonly held view is that historically centralized authority has become more despotic as society has become more complex. But even a cursory glance at ancient and medieval history demonstrates that this is not factually accurate. A more accurate view would be that while centralized authority in the state became more effective with greater technological and social sophistication, modern history has in fact been the record of the progressive rebellion against despotic state control. Moreover, the model for despotism is very ancient, deriving from the despotic authority in proto-androcratic society of the male as head of his household. Recent archeological data verify that from the first imposition of male dominance, this power was literally the power of life or death.[10]

Viewed from this larger perspective, splitting women's rights off from human rights may be seen to serve important systems maintenance functions in male dominant or patriarchal societies. The most obvious function is that by perpetuating the idea that the rights of women are of a different or lower order than the rights of "man," it serves to justify practices that do not accord women full and equal status. In other words, the segregation of women's rights from human rights both reflects and reinforces traditions where violations of the rights of women are not violations of either law or custom.

Beyond this, by preventing the formulation of a unified, and operationally effective, theory of international human rights, this double standard of thought has still another important systems maintenance function. It serves as a hidden but effective obstacle to fundamental systems change by preventing the application of the same standards to *all* human relations. This in turn serves to block the kinds of actions that could construct the psychological and sociological foundations for attaining the goals of the human rights movement: the creation of a social system where the human rights of *all* persons are fully recognized and respected.[11]

Cultural Traditions, the Public and Private Sphere, and Individual Rights

From the very beginning, the modern human rights movement has had to counter deeply entrenched patriarchal traditions. In the eighteenth, nineteenth, and in some places even the early twentieth century, the "divine right of kings" to rule was staunchly defended by religious authorities. In addition, secular philosophers like Edmund Burke argued that the doctrine of the "rights of man" would lead "to the utter subversion, not only of all government, in all modes, but all stable securities to

rational freedom, and all the rules and principles of morality itself."[12]

In the same way, the "women's rights" movement is to this day staunchly opposed by many religious authorities and some secular writers, for example George Gilder, who claims to represent "the man in the street." Once again, this opposition is on the ostensible grounds that women's rights are a threat to both family and social stability, as well as a subversion of the moral order.[13]

But when the double standard of human rights for women and men is analyzed in terms of its function for androcratic systems maintenance, the argument that women's rights are a threat to both our cultural traditions and family stability can be seen in a new light. The first thing that becomes apparent is that in this context the distinction between private or internal and public or political actions is merely another way of saying that in the private sphere of his home the male "head of household" *should* be in control—or that here the human rights of women *should not* be protected.

Certainly the right to privacy, or more precisely the right to protection from government interference with the right to privacy, is an important human right. The problem is that the terms *private sphere, family sphere,* and *right to privacy* have often been used interchangeably.

The term private sphere is generally applied to those areas of personal choice, action, and interpersonal relations where the government should not be able to interfere. But it is also often used to refer to the domestic or familial sphere. The question thus tends to become not whether there is interference with the individual right to privacy but whether there is government interference in the familial sphere.

By reframing the question it is possible to cut through some of this conceptual confusion, and to see how, while ostensibly protecting people's privacy, the distinction conventionally made between the public and the private sphere has often served as a means of preventing the application of developing human rights standards to the relations between men and women.

Let us return to the basic proposition that the aim of human rights activities is to secure protection for individual rights, and that one of these rights is the individual right to privacy. This right to privacy would include the right to freely choose with whom to speak and associate, with whom to have intimate (including sexual) relations, and, as long as it does not constitute a pattern of unlawful discrimination, the right to choose with whom to have, or not have, economic dealings. It would also include the right to freely choose whether to conceive or not to conceive, as well as the right to carry or not to carry a pregnancy to term.[14]

If we then look at the family as a social institution, the fundamental question is to what extent has society the right to interfere with the family in the interest of protecting individual rights, of which the right to privacy is one.

The critical rearticulation for legal theory is that the right to privacy is not synonymous with the right to noninterference with actions within the family. Nor is it synonymous with the right by the head of the household to governmental noninterference with his actions within the family. The right to privacy in both thought and action is rather an individual right, which like other *individual rights,* should be protected from government interference, be it inside or outside the context of the family.

In reality of course, all social systems, be they "primitive" or "civilized" societies, interfere with internal family affairs. They do so through the regulation, by law and custom, of marriage. They do so through the regulation of divorce. They further interfere in the family sphere through myriads of long accepted laws and customs, ranging all the way from those prohibiting incest to those regulating the inheritance of family-owned property.[15]

Indeed, the principle of noninterference with "family autonomy" is in actuality nowhere fully accepted. On the contrary, a universally established principle is that family relations are subject to both legal regulation and outside scrutiny. For example, the killing of one brother by another in the privacy of their home is regarded as a public offense in all modern codes of law.

In other words, the principle of noninterference with "family autonomy" is not consistently applied. It has in fact been applied in a very selective manner designed to maintain a particular type of familial (and social) organization: a male-headed, procreation-oriented patriarchal family in which women have few if any individual rights.[16]

In many American states as late as the nineteenth century (long after the Declaration of Independence proclaimed that all men have inalienable rights to life, liberty, and property), women were legally divested of all property rights. Economic transactions were to be carried out for women by their male guardians, and when a woman married (and marriage was most women's only option for social respectability and economic survival), her husband in effect became the legal guardian of both her person and her property. Upon marriage women were legally divested of any right to control property, including property they brought into the marriage. Also under the male's control were any wages his wife earned through her own labor. She did not have the right to sue for injuries to her own body, and any damages therefore, along with the right to her sexual services, became male property. And even today in many developing nations, women's property rights, along with their right to freely choose whom to marry or not to marry, as well as the right to divorce, are still extremely curtailed.[17]

Women's political rights have traditionally also been largely nonexistent. In the Cradle of Modern Democracy, the U.S. Constitution did not guarantee women the most elementary of all political rights, the right to vote, until 1920 (a half century after the Fifteenth Amendment granted that right to freed male slaves). And it was not until 1973 that the U.S. Supreme Court held that the most elementary of private rights, the right to decide whether to carry a pregnancy to term, was constitutionally protected under the right to privacy. Moreover, this right, as well as the right of both women and men to freely choose whether to conceive or not, is today under massive attack in the United States. And in many regions of the developing world (ironically often those with the highest poverty and, correlatively, birth rates), women have no right to reproductive freedom and are defined by both law and custom as literally male controlled mechanisms of reproduction.

A shocking case in point are the genital mutilations of women which still kill, maim, and blight the physical and psychological health of millions of women and little children every year in many parts of Asia and Africa today.[18] Unlike male circumcision, with which these practices are sometimes erroneously equated, these are not simply ceremonial cuttings of skin. They consist of cutting off the clitoris (designed to deprive women of sexual pleasure, and thus presumably the desire to "stray") and/or cutting off the labia and tightly sewing up the vaginal opening (making sexual intercourse a painful activity or actually impossible until a larger opening is again cut before marriage).[19]

Due to the challenge by women's rights advocates in many nations across the world, this once taboo subject has recently been exposed to public attention. As a result, a number of national leaders have condemned such practices and in some nations laws that prohibit them have been enacted.[20] But to date international human rights organizations have not taken a firm position on this important issue and have done little to encourage the passage and enforcement of such laws.

The ostensible basis for this inaction is that these are private rather than public practices and thus outside the purview of international human rights conventions. But clearly these practices are violations of a woman's right to privacy in the most fundamental sense: they are invasions of the basic human right to physical and sexual integrity. Were the practice in question the comparable act of cutting off a male's sexual parts, the international outcry surely would have been deafening.

International efforts to see that laws prohibiting torture and mutilation are enacted and enforced are a top human rights priority. Why should international efforts to encourage the enactment and enforcement of laws prohibiting the barbaric torture and mutilation of women be considered outside the purview of international human rights organizations?

One argument might be that genital mutilation is technically outside what is considered torture. In the conventional legal-political sense, torture is usually discussed in a different context.[21] It is condemned as an instrument of political oppression, a means of obtaining confessions or information, and above all, of exacting conformity and suppressing dissent. But while the practice of genital mutilation is deeply embedded in religious rites and/or ethnic customs, its essential purpose is to exact conformity, and, like the torture of political prisoners, it is a most effective means of breaking a person's spirit. In the realm of sexual politics, it is a means of perpetuating male power over—indeed, male ownership of—women. It is in fact an even more effective instrument of exacting conformity and suppressing dissent precisely because even the victim is socialized to accept and to expect it. Beyond this, it is a traumatic torture that not only causes death and immediate physical damage but also afflicts it survivors with painful physical and mental problems for the rest of their lives.

Despite all this, there are those who still argue that for the international human rights agencies to press for the enactment and enforcement of laws prohibiting genital mutilation would be improper interference with ethnic traditions, constituting merely one more form of "Western cultural imperialism." The fact is that non-Western women are today in the forefront of the movement to eradicate these practices.[22] Moreover, in the last analysis, the idea that one can justify genital mutilation in the name of respect for cultural traditions is not only horrifying, but ludicrous. All institutionalized behavior, including cannibalism and slavery, is cultural traditions. And surely no human rights advocate, or for that matter anyone else, would today dare to justify cannibalism or slavery—which were once also hallowed ethnic traditions in certain cultures—on cultural or traditional grounds.

The Underlying Issues

In the eighteenth century, when the modern human rights movement was still in its infancy, Western feminists challenged the medieval idea that a man's home is his castle where he is the sole and undisputed ruler. Today women from both the developed and developing world are demanding respect for the human rights of women—be it in the public or private sphere—and looking to international human rights organizations for support.

Explicitly challenging traditions that oppress and exploit women, the international women's movement is also implicitly challenging the idea that what a man does to members of his family is outside the purview of human rights protection. Nonetheless, this idea has been extremely resistant to change, even though it is as primitive and inhumane as the notion, specifically and properly rejected by human rights conventions, that human rights organizations may not interfere with what a government does to members of its nation. It has been a very effective way of maintaining an androcratic or patriarchal social order, since women's confinement to the home is most rigid precisely in those times and places where men most despotically rule in their homes.

The real issue is therefore one of priorities. As we have seen, it is clearly not whether human rights standards should apply to private as well as public acts. Rather, the issue is what *types* of private acts are and are not protected by the right to privacy and/or the principle of family autonomy. Even more specifically, the issue is whether violations of human rights within the family such as genital mutilation, wife beating, and other forms of violence designed to maintain patriarchal control should be within the purview of human rights theory and action, particularly in social systems where women have traditionally been confined to the private or familial sphere.

Reduced to its simplest and most basic terms, the underlying problem for human rights theory, as for most other fields of theory, is that the yardstick that has been developed for defining and measuring human rights has been based on the male as the norm.[23] The fact, of course, is that women are half (globally actually the majority) of the human population. The life experiences that are for either biological or traditional reasons typical for women are both similar to and different from those of males. The development of what may accurately be described as a theory of human rights therefore requires both a female and male yardstick for the protection of human rights.

From a systems perspective, the selective limitation of human rights standards to the public or political sphere and the double standard for women and men described by the distinction between "women's rights" and "human rights" may be seen as attempts to evade this basic issue. That this is the underlying problem may also be seen by taking a closer look at the related distinction between public or governmental and private or individual acts.[24]

Human rights organizations have consistently, and correctly, condemned governments that fail to protect their citizens from officially condoned acts of violence and torture as being in violation of human rights. In conformity with this position, the failure of governments to protect girls and women from the violence and torture of genital mutilation should logically also be viewed as violations of human rights. So also should be the failure of governments to provide protection from the terrorism of other traditional forms of male violence, such as wife battering and rape. For by failing to enact laws prohibiting such acts or failing to enforce such laws, a government *is* condoning acts of violence.

Moreover, if laws prohibiting incest or regulating inheritance are acceptable interferences in people's private lives, how can laws that would prohibit the sexual mutilation of female children or the beating of women be unacceptable interferences? There are still nations where a man's physical assault and battery of his wife as punishment for not obeying his orders is sanctioned by law.[25] Indeed, not so long ago such laws were part of the mainstream of Western tradition, with laws permitting a man to physically "punish" a "disobedient" wife only repealed in many American states during the nineteenth century. Moreover, even today in the United States and other "developed" nations, the police rarely arrest men for violating laws against wife battering—even though if they were to beat a stranger they would certainly be arrested. And in some "developing" nations, presumably following Islamic law, the police actually bring women back by force to homes they have fled because of abuse![26]

Laws permitting men to beat women who do not obey them are as much violations of human rights as would be laws permitting police beatings of those who fail to obey their governments. And the right of a woman to be free of male violence and brutality is as much a human right as the right of a man to enjoy freedom from fear of police brutality and violence.

Here again, the real issue is not whether ethnic traditions should, or should not, be within the purview of human rights theory and action. It is rather whether—be it in the private or the public sphere—protection of the human rights of women should be a top priority.

That this is the underlying issue becomes strikingly evident in light of yet another generally ignored fact. This is that the failure of human rights theory to include traditional practices that violate the human rights of women does not in reality hinge on the distinction between private and public action. There are actually many areas of direct government action where the denial to women of basic human rights is explicitly condoned and openly enforced by governments.

A notable example is segregation by sex. South African apartheid, or the government-enforced segregation of blacks and whites, is universally and properly considered a basic and urgent human rights issue. But the segregation of women and men is enforced by the governments of many nations. And while it affects many more millions of people, and is certainly no less urgent and major a human rights issue, the still widespread segregation based on sex has as yet not been condemned by any of the major human rights organizations.

The "separate but equal" policy that was a tradition in the American South was in the 1950s exposed as a smokescreen for racial discrimination that unlawfully curtailed blacks' opportunities in education and other spheres of life.[27] The "separate but equal" policies of governments that continue to segregate men and women in education and other spheres of life is no less a smokescreen for gender based discrimination. There is ample documentation of this fact. For example, in Saudi Arabia, which rigidly segregates the sexes, only 19 percent of women are literate as compared to 44 percent of men. Similarly in Pakistan the ratio is 22 to 44 percent, in Algeria it is 33 to 69 percent, in Egypt it is 30 to 59 percent, and in Iran it is 39 to 62 percent.[28]

On the same grounds that the segregation of blacks and whites is universally condemned, the segregation of women and men must be universally condemned. Human rights advocates loudly and properly reject the idea that blacks are too primitive and savage to have the same freedom as whites. But where are the objections to the teaching, formally incorporated into the curriculum of no less an institution than the University of Teheran, that women are weak and dangerous and must therefore be controlled by men?[29] Where are the objections to the requirement, officially enforced at the University of Teheran and other schools that mold the minds of millions of people in Africa and Asia, that females may not share classrooms with males? Isn't this the same abhorrent practice as the former separation of white and black students in the American South? Why, if human rights advocates vigorously condemn apartheid (the splitting off from the mainstream of society those who happen to be born black) do they not also vigorously condemn the splitting off from the mainstream of society those who happen to have been born female?

Because the examples from the Middle East are most striking, the temptation may again be to frame the issue in regional and/or religious terms. Segregation by sex, however, is to varying degrees a universal problem, characteristic of Eastern and Western secular and religious societies. It is instructive, and sobering, to remember that sex segregation was practiced in U.S. universities until World War II. Moreover, a universal remnant from earlier and more severe forms of sex segregation in the West is the segregation of jobs into "men's" and "women's" work, with any work assigned to women also assigned lower pay and status, regardless of requirements of technical skill, intellectual ability, or moral sensitivity.[30] In other words, framing the problem in ethnic or religious terms veils its function of androcratic systems maintenance.

The problems behind sex segregation and other institutionalized practices that deny women equal protection from discrimination and oppression are of course not only legal. But examples such as the U.S. Supreme Court case of *Brown v. Board of Education* demonstrate that laws are the floor on which social progress rests.

International law that fully integrates "women's rights" into "human rights" would establish the foundation for a just and humane world order.

This is by no means to say that women's rights must not be separately, and vigorously, advocated. Quite the contrary, just as black rights have to be viewed as a particularly urgent category of human rights, women's rights require similar attention. Indeed, the full integration of women's rights and human rights hinges on a vigorous international women's rights movement.

A Systems View of Human Rights

A first major step in the modern human rights movement aimed at the top portion of the patriarchal pyramid was the successful challenge to the "divine right" of kings to rule.[31] The second major step is the successful challenge of the "divine right" of men to rule. Largely because this second challenge has not yet been successful, the modern struggle for human rights remains incomplete. It has left the bottom part of the patriarchal pyramid, the foundations upon which a hierarchic and authoritarian system rests, in place.

Thanks to the cumulative effect of the nineteenth and twentieth century feminist movement, which is now spreading to all parts of the globe through the First United Nations Decade for Women, this hitherto invisible obstacle to the attainment of human rights for all peoples is increasingly being recognized. But to date, this recognition has remained largely peripheral to the mainstream of human rights theory. As a result, the human rights movement and the women's rights movement have remained generally segregated, with severely deleterious consequences for the human rights of *both* women and men.

For women, the consequences of a traditionally imposed second place, be it in the family or in the broader social, economic, and political spheres, have been, and continue to be, severe infringements of the most basic of human rights: the rights to life, liberty, and property. So severe is the infringement of women's property rights that, even though women perform two-thirds of the world's work hours, globally women own only one-hundredth as much property as men.[32] The infringement of women's right to liberty is also still commonplace in many parts of the world. The extent to which women's freedom of movement is interfered with is perhaps most dramatically illustrated by the Eastern practice of *purdah*. While for many women this is an effective form of house arrest, it is still generally viewed by Westerners as no more than a quaint ethnic tradition, much as the crippling footbinding that almost totally restricted the liberty of Chinese women was once seen. Similarly, while laws and customs that restrict women's life opportunities are still so numerous as to be almost ubiquitous, and have throughout history been the cause of tremendous suffering, indignities, and injustices, they are still so generally taken for granted that they are often merely considered "women's lot in life."

Even the killing of women—through female infanticide or through the culturally approved "family honor" murders of "errant" daughters or wives—has traditionally been sanctioned in many parts of the globe.[33] Moreover, through systematic discrimination in food and health care allocation, girls have often been subject to socially sanctioned criminal neglect. For example, a recent Bangladesh survey found that infant girls were 21 percent more likely than boys to die in their first year of life.[34] And it is estimated that in the Indian subcontinent boys outnumber girls among hospitalized children by approximately fifty to one even though malnutrition has been found to be four or five times more common among girls.[35] So the cost to women of the still prevailing double standard for the rights of women and men has all too often been the cost of life itself.

But as severe as the consequences have

been for women, the consequences of diminishing the opportunities and abridging the rights of half the population have been no less serious for society at large.[36] Perhaps the grimmest, though still generally ignored, case in point is the effect of sexually discriminatory practices on health.

It is a well known fact that in many parts of the world women's right to equal access to food is severely abridged by practices ranging from food taboos restricting women's protein intake to the custom of women eating after they have cooked for and served the male family members. A less well known fact is that, according to World Health Organizations figures, no less than half of all women and 60 percent of pregnant women in Third World nations suffer from nutritional anemia.[37] Since the health of a pregnant woman affects the health of her unborn child, the predictable result for society at large is the birth of children of *both* sexes who are physically, and often also mentally, impaired. In other words, largely as a result of the so-called women's issue of traditions that effectively deprive women of equal access to food, the health and well being of entire populations is severely damaged.[38]

Last, but not least, are the disastrous consequences of the double standard of human rights for women and men for the attainment of the just social order that is the goal of the modern struggle of human rights. If we look at the totality of our social institutions from a systems perspective, focusing on the relationship between the various parts of the social system, it becomes apparent that the major obstacle that at every turn has blocked or reversed the movement for human rights is that the rights of one half of humanity have not been effectively addressed.

How we structure the most fundamental of all human relations—the relation of the female and male halves of humanity—has profound implications for how we structure all human relations.[39] As John Stuart Mill wrote over one hundred years ago in a work that is still generally relegated to the women's ghetto of feminist studies, only when "the most fundamental of the social relations is placed under the rule of equal justice" can a just society be realized.[40] As long as one set of rules and public policies continues to be applied to one half of humanity and another set to the other, the very foundation for the protection of human rights, that *all* human beings have certain inalienable rights, remains fatally undermined.[41]

Viewed in systems terms, the right to be free of tyrannical violence and a social organization that sanctions violence in the most intimate social relations—between women and men—are totally incompatible. This seemingly self-evident fact has recently been verified by the author in a new study of society from a gender holistic perspective, that is, an approach that takes into full account the experiences of both the female and male halves of humanity. This study indicates that there is an integral relationship between all forms of male socialization and violence. It also shows that more rigidly male dominant societies tend to be more rigidly repressive of both women and men. Moreover, it confirms that violence or the threat of violence plays a critical part in the maintenance of a male dominant or patriarchal social organization, where the ideal for social relations is imaged in the form of a pyramid, with a strongman ruler and/or a small male elite ruling from the top, and all men in turn ruling over women and children.[42]

A Major Step for Human Rights

As the First United Nations Decade for Women evidences, women all over the world are today asserting that the same human rights standards that are already widely applied to the relations between men and men should apply to the relations between women and men. One result has been the UN Convention on the Elimination of All Forms of Discrimination Against Women, adopted shortly before the midpoint of the Decade. Because it expressly addressed violations of the human rights of women, the Convention is a potentially pivotal turning point in the human rights movement.

The Convention on the Elimination of All Forms of Discrimination Against Women was the first UN document to recognize expressly that, despite other international conventions against discrimination, violations of the human rights of half of humanity still remain generally ignored. It was also the first UN instrument to deal comprehensively with all aspects of women's human rights, to establish standards that are binding on states parties (i.e., ratifying nations), and to set up the machinery for exerting pressure on national governments to abide by these standards. In specific, although still largely unnoted, respects, the Convention addressed some of the major theoretical barriers to a unified, and operationally effective, theory of human rights.

Article 1 expressly addresses the traditional distinction between the public or external and private or internal sphere. It defines the term "discrimination against women" as "any distinction, exclusion, or restriction made on the basis of sex which has the effect or purpose of impairing or nullifying the recognition, enjoyment, or exercise by women, *irrespective of their marital status, on a basis of equality of men and women, of human rights and fundamental freedoms in the political, economic, social, cultural, civil, or any other field.*"[43] In other words, it calls for the international recognition of the human rights of women *both* inside and outside their traditional private or familial sphere.

Article 16 goes even further, specifically stating that "States Parties shall take all appropriate measures to eliminate discrimination against women in all matters relating *to marriage and family relations*" (emphasis added). It also requires that states parties shall ensure women traditionally "private" rights, such as the "rights to decide freely and responsibly on the number and spacing of their children and to have access to the information, education, and means to enable them to exercise these rights." It requires recognition and enforcement of women's right "to choose a family name" and "a profession and an occupation." And in requiring protection of women's rights of "ownership, acquisition, management, administration, enjoyment, and disposition of property," it directly challenges the male's economic control of the family.[44]

Of major significance is that the Convention expressly addresses the traditional justification of denying human rights to women on the basis of ethnic customs or practices. Article 5 states that:

States Parties shall take all appropriate measures:

(a) *To modify the social and cultural patterns of conduct of men and women, with a view to achieving the limitation of prejudices and customary and all other practices which are based on the idea of the inferiority or the superiority of either of the sexes or on stereotyped roles for men and women.*[45]

The importance of this provision cannot be overestimated. As ungenerous as the law has traditionally been to women, at least in modern times violations of human rights of women have remained far more entrenched in attitudes and customs. Despite the adage that morality cannot be legislated, habits of thinking and acting can be and have been changed by law, particularly if these laws have strong and consistent official support.

But the Convention on the Elimination of All Forms of Discrimination Against Women not only provides essential guidelines for national policies. Of equal importance is that it constitutes the hitherto missing link for the construction of an internally consistent theory of human rights that expressly rejects the traditional exclusion of "women's rights" from the purview of international human rights activities.

This is a critical step toward the completion of the modern struggle for human rights.

The exclusion of "women's rights" from the purview of international efforts aimed at protecting human rights has not only helped maintain severe infringements of the human rights of women worldwide but has also subverted and undermined the entire human rights movement. The ratification of the Convention by all world governments must therefore be a major policy goal of international human rights organizations.

It is often argued that change has to come from inside. Pressure for change is indeed mounting from inside in most, if not all, nations on earth—as evidenced by the First United Nations Decade for Women, with its three major international conferences and grass-roots participations by women of all races, creeds, and nationalities. The critical point is that time and time again these women have expressed the need for outside support because of enormous internal efforts to suppress the forces working from inside for humanistic social change. And this is precisely what the international human rights movement is designed to provide.

Organizations such as Amnesty International are beginning to focus more attention on the rights of female political prisoners. Vigorous support by international human rights organizations for the ratification of the Convention on the Elimination of All Forms of Discrimination Against Women and the reformulation of human rights theory to explicitly include the female half of humanity are the next logical steps. This will not only accelerate urgently needed humanistic social change affecting one half of the human population but also lay the essential foundations toward a fully integrated and effective movement for international human rights.

Forward or Backward

It should be enough to say that the full recognition of the rights of half of humanity is essential to finally put an end to the suffering and degradation of women and female children.

201

But unfortunately it is not enough. It has long been said, and fallen largely on deaf ears.

One of the many illustrations is the lack of attention given to the well documented practice of female sexual slavery. The 1974 INTERPOL (General Secretariat of the International Police Organization) report to the United Nations documented South American, Mid Eastern, Asian, European, and African networks that traffic—and often sell—women into prostitution and other sexual markets. The UNESCO report in 1975 on prostitution "hotels" in Europe was another horrifying documentation of the torture and imprisonment of women in prostitution. Nonetheless, there was no follow-up to either.[46]

Similarly, widespread practices such as bride-payment, forced marriages, seclusion and veiling, genital mutilation, and polygamy—all designed to establish, transfer, and maintain male ownership of women—have yet to be addressed by international human rights organizations.[47] The United Nations has adopted a number of conventions specifically condemning slavery, or the ownership of one human being by another, and any form of slave trade. That female sexual slavery, which in one form or another affects a very large proportion of the world's population, is in violation of these conventions has clearly been articulated. As Fran Hosken writes, "a man claiming to own the body and labor of another man would be instantly accused of slavery. Is it not a human rights violation if a man claims to own the labor, indeed the bodies of the female members of his family—as is the case in many traditional societies?"[48] Nonetheless, these massive violations of the basic human right to liberty are effectively ignored, dismissed as violations of "women's rights."

But while until now neither appeals to reason or compassion have succeeded, the time may be ripe for a change. Perhaps never before in modern history has there been such a massive

attack on human rights. This attack is global, transcending such conventional ideological labels as Right or Left, Eastern or Western, secular or religious.[49] What may turn the tide and lead into a new era for the human rights of both women and men is that the battle lines are increasingly being drawn around so-called women's issues.

All over the world today those working to push us back to "the good old days" before the rights of either women or men were a social and political issue, advocate a return to traditions that maintain the sexual and social subjugation of women. In the United States, the far Right has spent millions to fight the Equal Rights Amendment to the U.S. Constitution as well as reproductive freedom of choice, pay equity, educational equity, and even shelters for battered women and laws against child and wife beating, because they would weaken male rule in the home. Similarly, in many Third World nations, those who display the greatest indifference to existing international conventions on human rights see women's rights as a prime target. For example, for the Ayatollah Khomeini, whose tyrannical regime chronically violated human rights conventions, the return of women to their proper or subservient place is a top priority.[50]

But for many human rights leaders, women's issues are still at best secondary. When violations of the human rights of women are brought up, a standard retort is that as long as men on this earth are tortured, mutilated, killed, or unjustly imprisoned, how can they be expected to deal with anything else? The problem seems to be more lack of perception than lack of good will. Under the double standard of "human rights" and "women's rights," the killings of "errant" women or "unsatisfactory" brides by members of their own families in Moslem nations and India, the imprisonment of women through *purdah* and other traditions confining them to virtual house-arrest and generally restricting their freedom of movement, and the well-documented barbarism of mutilating and torturing millions of little girls and women through "female circumcision" are somehow not perceived as mutilations, tortures, killings, and imprisonments that brutally violate human rights. Rather, they are regarded as regrettable aspects of the situation of women in places where different customs prevail.[51]

It is ironic that the systems connection between "women's rights" and "human rights" is, in both theory and action, more often recognized by those working against, rather than for,

human rights. And it is also extremely dangerous to the human rights of *both* women and men.

The recognition that women's rights are the leading edge of human rights is both operationally and logically the prerequisite for the kinds of actions required to lay the foundations for a just social order. A unified theory of human rights encompassing both halves of humanity is essential if a basic respect for human rights is to become firmly rooted. Only then can the unfinished struggle for equal justice for *all*—the struggle for human rights—be completed.

Notes

1. Convention on the Elimination of All Forms of Discrimination Against Women, art. 3, G.A. Res. 34/180, U.N. Doc. A/Res/34/180 (1980). For an overview of the traditional UN approach to the human rights of women, see Laura Reanda, "Human Rights and Women's Rights: The United Nations Approach," *Human Rights Quarterly* 3 (Spring 1981): 11–31. See also H. Pietila, *What the United Nations Means to Women* (Geneva: United Nations Non-Governmental Liaison Service, 1985).

2. See, e.g., the Universal Declaration of Human Rights, *adopted* 10 December 1948, G.A. Res. 217A (III), U.N. Doc. A/810 (1948); the Convention on the Political Rights for Women, *opened for signature* 31 March 1953, *entered into force* 7 July 1954, 27 U.S.T. 8289, T.I.A.S. No. 8289, 193 U.N.T.S. 135; the Convention on the Nationality of Married Women, *adopted* 29 January 1957, *entered into force* 11 August 1958, 309 U.N.T.S. 65; the Declaration on the Elimination of Discrimination Against Women, G.A. Res. 2263, 22 U.N. GAOR Supp. (No. 16), U.N. Doc. A/6716 (1967); the Proclamation of Teheran, U.N. Doc. A/CONF.32/41 (1968); the Convention for the Suppression of the Traffic in Persons and the Exploitation of the Prostitution of Others, *adopted* 2 December 1949, *entered into force* 25 July 1951, 96 U.N.T.S. 271; and the Supplementary Convention on the Abolition of Slavery, the Slave Trade, and Institutions and Practices Similar to Slavery, *signed* 7 September 1956, *entered into force* 30 April 1957, 18 U.S.T. 3201, T.I.A.S. No. 6418, 266 U.N.T.S. 3.

3. See also 1979 State of the World Women's Report, United Nations; and *Report of the World Conference to Review and Appraise the Achievements of the United*

Nations Decade for Women: Equality, Development, and Peace, U.N. Doc. A/CONF.94/35 (1980).

4. See, e.g., John Locke, "An Essay Concerning the True Original Extent and End of Civil Government" and J. J. Rousseau, "From the Social Contract," in *The World's Great Thinkers: Man and the State,* ed. S. Commins and R. Linscott (New York: Random House, 1947); and the Preamble to the U.S. Declaration of Independence.

5. See J. J. Rousseau, note 4 above. A little publicized sidelight on Rousseau's famous misogyny is provided by historian Linda Kerber, who notes that his sado-masochistic sexual tastes may have given Rousseau an additional stake in perpetuating the submission of women. See Linda Kerber, *Women and The Republic: Intellect and Ideology in Revolutionary America* (Chapel Hill, N.C.: University of North Carolina Press, 1980).

6. For example, at the first United States Women's Rights Convention in 1848, Elizabeth Cady Stanton adopted the U.S. Declaration of Independence as a "women's rights manifesto" by adding to it two critical words: "We hold these truths to be self-evident: that all and men *and women* are created equal; that they are endowed by their Creator with certain inalienable rights; that among these are life, liberty, and the pursuit of happiness." Thus, in the same year that Marx and Engels issued the Communist Manifesto, demanding economic rights for the "working man," three hundred persons assembled in the Wesleyan Chapel at Seneca Falls, New York, to assert that women are entitled not only to economic but also political and social rights; "to insist that they have immediate admission to all the rights and privileges which belong to them as citizens of the United States." "Seneca Falls Declaration of Sentiments," in *Feminism: The Essential Historical Writings*, ed. Miriam Schneir (New York: Random House, 1972).

7. For detailed information of how the human rights of women have been split off from the mainstream of the international human rights movement, see the special issue on "Symposium: Women and International Human Rights," guest ed. F. P. Hosken, *Human Rights Quarterly* 3 (Spring 1981).

8. A distinction should be made between intervention by another nation to protect or advance its own interests, which is usually of a military character, and non-military attempts to intervene by international agencies for the protection of human rights. Since the French Revolution, there have been explicit statements by governments operating under a particular system (e.g., monarchies) that one nation may interfere in the internal affairs of another during times of threatened social change, particularly in cases of revolution, whenever a "legitimate" government is thereby threatened.

9. W. B. Blackstone, *Commentaries*, 19th London ed. (Philadelphia: Lippincott Co., 1908): 366.

10. Proto-androcratic describes a prototypical male dominant, violent, and hierarchical social organization. In Europe archeological data indicate that the shift from a matrilineal, matrifocal, and generally peaceful and egalitarian society to a patrilineal, patrifocal, and androcratic society began circa 4400 B.C. with the first wave of Indo-European (Kurgan) invasions. The archeological record evidences a dramatic change. For example, there is the first appearance of "chieftain graves" and what archeologists call "suttee burials." Here among the "funerary gifts" we find sacrificed women along with weapons and other possessions of the deceased, attesting to the continuation of the male's absolute power even after death. See, e.g., Marija Gimbutas, "The First Wave of Eurasian Steppe Pastoralists into Copper Age Europe," *Journal of Indo-European Studies* 5 (Winter 1977): 277–338. See also Riane Eisler with the contribution of David Loye, *The Chalice and the Blade: Our History, Our Future* (San Francisco: Harper & Row, 1987), chap. 4.

11. See, e.g., Riane Eisler, "Human Rights: The Unfinished Struggle," *International Journal of Women's Studies* 6 (September/October 1983): 326–335; Eisler, *The Chalice and the Blade*, note 10 above.

12. Edmund Burke, quoted in Alburey Castel, *An Introduction to Modern Philosophy* (New York: Macmillan, 1946): 425.

13. George F. Gilder, *Wealth and Poverty* (New York: Basic Books, 1981); see also Riane Eisler, *The Equal Rights Handbook: What ERA Means to Your Life, Your Rights, and the Future* (New York: Avon Books, 1978).

14. This is not to say that these rights have traditionally been protected or that even now they are uniformly recognized. For example, laws forbidding interracial marriage were once commonplace in the American South and still exist in some parts of the world. Freedom of speech and assembly are severely curtailed in many nations. So also is reproductive freedom of choice even though, as U.S. Supreme Court Justice Harry A. Blackmun recently wrote, "few decisions are more personal and intimate, more properly private or more basic to individual dignity and autonomy than a woman's decision . . . whether to end her pregnancy." *Thornburgh v. American College of Obstetricians and Gynecologists*, 105 S. Ct. 2169 (1986).

15. Riane Eisler, *Dissolution: No-Fault Divorce, Marriage, and the Future of Women* (New York: McGraw-Hill, 1977).

16. Ibid.

17. For an excellent overview of how under both law and custom women continue to be deprived of property rights, see F. P. Hosken, "Women and Property," *Development Forum* (October 1984). Under Hosken's direction, Women's International Network (WIN) is currently developing a detailed program and budget for a worldwide investigation of women's property/land rights, which will be a future International Research and Training Institute for the Advancement of Women (INSTRAW) project.

18. See, e.g., *Sudan: National Study on the Epidemiology of Female Circumcision*, the first systematic countrywide investigation of genital mutilation by Dr. Asma El Dareer, Department of Community Medicine, University of Khartoum, 1980; F. P. Hosken, *The Hosken Report: Genital and Sexual Mutilation of Females* (Lexington, Mass.: WIN News 1982, 1984): 38–39, the first comprehensive work to bring these practices to public attention; A. G. Selassie, M. Desta, and Z. Negesh, "Harmful Traditional Practices Affecting the Health of Women and Children in Ethiopia," report funded by UNICEF/AAO Ethiopia, P.O. Box 1169, Addis Ababa, Ethiopia; Odile Botti, "The Battle Against Excisions by Africans: A Survey of Actions in Three West African Countries," *Marie Claire* (November 1985); Salah Abu Bakr, *The Effect of Vulval Mutilation on the Nerve Supply: Ana-*

tomical Considerations, Ministry of Health, Sudan (the monograph unequivocally establishes that these operations deprive women of ability to feel genital sensation); Renée Saurel, *L'Enteree Vive* (Geneve-Paris: Editions Slatkine, 1981); numerous other materials including *Enaba, Aziza Wa Abeer,* the 1980 documentary film on women's lives and clitoridectomy, by Dr. Laila Abou-Saif, an Egyptian filmmaker; and the excellent up-to-date reports in the Section on Genital and Sexual Mutilations of Females that appear in the quarterly *WIN News,* published by F. P. Hosken. For an important article examining the human rights issues involved, see F. P. Hosken, "Female Genital Mutilations and Human Rights," *Feminist Issues* 1 (Summer 1981): 3–23.

19. Among African nations that have recently begun to take measures against the continuation of genital mutilations are Egypt, Kenya, and Sudan, where in 1979 the Khartoum Seminar organized by the World Health Organization (WHO) was held and recommendations were made to eradicate these practices. Since these "operations," which are sometimes fatal, are being exported to Europe along with Moslem and African immigrants, a number of European nations, including France, Sweden, and Great Britain, have also recently begun to address these practices. M. Abdou Kiouf, President of Senegal, Thomas Sankara, Chief of State of Burkina Faso, Mathieu Kerkou, Chief of State of Benin, Moussa Traore, President of Mali, and Hassan Gouled Aptridom, President of Djibouti, have also spoken out against these practices. Quoted in *WIN News* 12 (Spring 1986): 31.

20. Ibid.

21. The Convention Against Torture and Other Cruel, Inhuman, or Degrading Treatment or Punishment, U.N. Doc. A/39/708 (1984) [????] 1:

> For the purpose of this Convention, the term "torture" means any act by which severe pain or suffering, whether physical or mental, is intentionally inflicted on a person for such purposes as obtaining from him or a third person information or a confession, punishing him for an act he or a third person has committed or is suspected of having committed, or intimidating or coercing him or a third person, or for any reason based on discrimination of any kind, when such pain or suffering is inflicted by or at the instigation of or with the consent or acquiescence of a public official or other person acting in an official capacity. It does not include pain or suffering arising only from, inherent in or incidental to lawful sanctions.

22. For example, at the 1985 UN End of the Decade for Women Conference in Nairobi, Kenya, attended by the author, some of the clearest voices against genital mutilation were those of Muslim women. Even among the still rigidly male dominated Masai tribes of Kenya, women are now beginning to reject these "traditional practices."

23. For an excellent recent article stressing this point and the problems it creates for "equality theory," see Lucinda M. Finley, "Transcending Equality Theory: A Way Out of the Maternity and the Workplace Debate," *Columbia Law Review* 86 (October 1986): 1118–81.

24. See, e.g., Riane Eisler, "Human Rights: The Unfinished Struggle," note 11 above; F. P. Hosken, "Editorial: Women's Rights and Human Rights," *WIN News* 10 (Spring 1984): 1–2. As Hosken writes, "An examination of human rights on the global level is meaningless unless it is based on the examination of human rights on the family level, and between family members, women and men."

25. For example, in Kenya a bill that would have required reforms in polygamy and traditional violence against women was shelved by an overwhelming majority in 1979. One of the legislators, Kimunai arap Soi, charged that the bill would make it impossible to teach wives "manners" by beating them and that the proposed legislation was "very un-African." Another opponent, Wafula Wabuge, contended in opposition to the bill that African women loved their men more when they were slapped, "for then the wives call you darling." *Time Magazine* report quoted in *WIN News* 5 (Autumn 1979): 42.

26. For continuing reports see *WIN News* regular section on Women and Violence. For a historical view of American law see Riane Eisler, *Dissolution: No-Fault Divorce, Marriage, and the Future of Women,* note 15 above.

27. See, e.g., *Brown v. Board of Education,* 347 U.S. 483 (1954).

28. Ruth Leger Sivard, *Women: A World Survey* (Washington, D.C.: World Priorities, 1985).

29. *WIN News* 9 (Autumn 1983): 42.

30. A classic work on this subject is Carolyn Bird, *Born Female* (New York: Pocket Books, 1968).

31. Even before this, Renaissance humanists attacked the traditional body of intolerance of Western society (particularly its religious dogmatism). This opened the debate that made it possible during the Enlightenment to frontally challenge the divine right of kings.

32. UN *1985 State of the World Women's Report* (Oxford, U.K.: compiled and written on behalf of the United Nations by New International Publications, 1985). See also note 17.

33. For example, a 3 January 1981 story in the *Journal-American* reported:

> Unmarried pregnant Arab girls who may face death at the hands of their relatives are escaping by "underground railway" from the tradition-bound West Bank of the Jordan River to Europe. Families frequently kill such girls in the name of honor. . . . Even modern societies in countries like Lebanon and Egypt still do not deal harshly with perpetrators of so-called "honor killings.". . . "It's impossible to get exact figures," a physician said, "but I would estimate that there is one honor killing a week in the West Bank. . . . The girls usually are poisoned or burned to death and the murder made to look accidental," he said. He described some cases: "A father in Hebron, south of Jerusalem, reports that his daughter killed herself by jumping into a well. An autopsy shows she was poisoned. . . . [A] 17-year-old girl with burns over most of her body and face has a miscarriage in a hospital. Her family says a kerosene heater tipped over accidentally."

Excerpt reprinted in *WIN News* 7 (Spring 1981): 52.

34. See, e.g., *Review and Appraisal: Health and Nutrition*, World Conference to Review and Appraise the Achievements of the United Nations Decade for Women, Nairobi, Kenya, July 1985, U.N. Doc. A/CONF.116/5/Add.3; "Women in Food Production, Food Handling and Nutrition with Special Emphasis on Africa," study by the United Nations Protein-Calorie Advisory Food Group, *PAG Bulletin* III (September/December 1977) as well as the latest PAG report summarized in *WIN News* 12 (Summer 1986), and Fran Hosken, *The Hosken Report* section on Women and Development (see note 18 above). Further information may be obtained from Women's International Network, 187 Grant Street, Lexington, MA 02173.

35. *Review and Appraisal: Health and Nutrition*, note 34 above.

36. Eisler, "Human Rights: The Unfinished Struggle," note 11 above; Eisler, *The Chalice and the Blade*, note 10 above.

37. Sivard, note 28 above.

38. Eisler, *The Chalice and the Blade*, note 10 above; Riane Eisler and V. Csanyi, *Human Biology and Social Structure*, work in progress.

39. Eisler, *The Chalice and the Blade*, note 10 above.

40. John Stuart Mill, "The Subjection of Women," in *The Feminist Papers*, ed. Alice S. Rossi (New York: Bantam Books, 1973), 238.

41. Eisler, "Human Rights: The Unfinished Struggle," note 11 above; Eisler, *The Chalice and the Blade*, note 10 above.

42. See, e.g., Riane Eisler and David Loye, "The 'Failure' of Liberalism: A Reassessment of Ideology from a New Feminine-Masculine Perspective," *Political Psychology* 4 (June 1983): 375–91; Eisler, *The Chalice and the Blade*, note 10 above; Riane Eisler and David Loye, "Peace and Feminist Thought: New Directions," *World Encyclopedia of Peace* (London: Pergamon Press, in press); Riane Eisler, "Violence and Male Dominance: The Ticking Time Bomb," *Humanities in Society* 7 (Winter, Spring 1984): 3–18.

43. Convention on the Elimination of All Forms of Discrimination Against Women, art. 1, U.N. Doc. A/34/46 (1980) (emphasis added).

44. Ibid., art. 16.

45. Ibid., art 5 (emphasis added).

46. Kathleen Barry, "Female Sexual Slavery: Understanding the International Dimensions of Women's Oppression," *Human Rights Quarterly* 3 (Spring 1981): 45.

47. Ibid., 44–45.

48. Fran P. Hosken, "Editorial: Women's Rights and Human Rights," note 24 above. For a good overview of the "invisibility" of these human rights violations, see "Symposium: Women and International Human Rights," *Human Rights Quarterly* 3 (Spring 1981).

49. See, e.g., Riane Eisler, "Women's Rights and Human Rights," *The Humanist* (November/December 1980): 24–29; Riane Eisler and David Loye, "The Failure of Liberalism: A Reassessment of Ideology from a New Feminine-Masculine Perspective," note 42 above.

50. See, e.g., Riane Eisler, "Women's Rights and Human Rights," note 49 above.

51. Ibid.

Women, Development, and Population: Highlights from the 1989 State of World Population Report

by Dr. Nafis Sadik

Women are at the heart of development. They control most of the non-money economy (subsistence agriculture, bearing and raising children, domestic labor) and take an important part in the money economy (trading, the "informal sector," wage employment). Everywhere in the world women have two jobs—around the home and outside it.

Much of this work is unrecognized and those who do it can expect no support. Their health suffers, their work suffers, their children suffer. Development itself is held back as a result.

This report demonstrates some of the costs of ignoring the needs of women: uncontrolled population growth, high infant and child mortality, a weakened economy, ineffective agriculture, a deteriorating environment, a generally divided society and a poorer quality of life for all. For girls and women it means unequal opportunities, a higher level of risk, and a life determined by fate and the decisions of others rather than choice.

Many women, especially in developing countries, have few choices in life outside marriage and children. They tend to have large families because that is expected of them. Investing in women means widening their choice of strategies and reducing their dependence on children for status and support. Family planning is one of the most important investments, because it represents the freedom from which other freedoms flow.

Investments in women include, besides family planning, "social investment," services such as health and education. The report demonstrates that such services help women to do much better what they are already doing and open the door to new possibilities.

But investing in women must go beyond such services, and remove the barriers preventing them from exploring their full potential. That means granting them equal access to land, to credit, to rewarding employment—as well as establishing their effective personal and political rights.

Making the necessary changes means recognizing women not only as wives and mothers, but as vital and valuable members of society. It means that women themselves must take power in their own hands to shape the direction of their lives and the development of their communities. It means rethinking development plans from the start so that women's abilities, rights, and needs are taken into account at every stage—so that women's status and security are derived from their entire contribution to society, rather than only from childbearing. Few would argue against providing women with better welfare services; but making investment in women a development priority will require a major change in attitudes to development not only by developing countries but also by financial and lending institutions. Under increasing economic pressure in the last four years, thirty-seven of the poorest countries have cut health spending by 50 percent, and education by 25 percent. This burden falls hardest on the poor, and hardest of all on poor women.

The challenge for those who believe that women's contribution is central to development and that investment in women should take priority, even in societies under severe economic stress, is to make an irresistible case for the change.

Change of some kind cannot be avoided. In the face of population growth, the urban explosion, the developing environmental crisis, escalating international debt, and growing poverty in many of the poorest of the developing countries, many authorities agree that some kind of fundamental rethinking is long overdue. The concept of "sustainable development," in which human and natural resources are brought into a dynamic equilibrium, is one response. Women have a central part in any system of sustainable development.

Population Update

Currently 5.2 billion, world population will increase by over 90 million each year until the end of the century. All but six million of each year's increase will live in developing countries. According to the United Nations, the population at the end of this century will be about 6.25 billion; about 8.5 billion by 2025. It may stop growing at 10 billion, about double its present size, perhaps a century from now.

The projection is quite optimistic: it assumes that fertility in the developing world as a whole will drop by a third in the next thirty to forty years. This in turn assumes that a very large number of women in developing countries will start to use family planning in the next two decades.

If this does not happen, the United Nations estimates that population will continue to increase, by large numbers and for longer. Their less optimistic projection, for example, shows a population already approaching 10 billion by 2025: by that time Africa's population would be nearly 2 billion and Asia's nearly 5.5 billion, bigger than the population of the whole world today. The eventual stable total could be 14 billion.

These figures alone, and their implications for the global future, should be enough to make it clear that the population crisis is a matter for action now, not in the next century. By then it will be too late.

Recommendations

Sustainable development can only be achieved with the full and equal participation of women; when population, environmental, and development linkages are adequately translated into policies and programs; and when social sectors are given equal priority with economic growth.

These recommendations are addressed mainly to governments. However, international organizations and non-governmental organizations also have a wide responsibility in this area.

1. Documenting and publicizing women's vital contribution to development.

There is still a shortage of vital quantitative and qualitative information on women. National data collection systems do not yet accurately document women's contribution to development. All countries should:

- Ensure that national statistics—on employment, mortality, morbidity, etc.—are disaggregated by sex;
- Investigate and quantify women's unpaid work and their work in the informal sector;
- Assign an economic value to women's unpaid work;
- Ensure timely and regular availability of socioeconomic indicators on women;
- Provide the widest possible audience with accurate and full information on women's productive and reproductive responsibilities.

2. *Increasing the productivity of women and lessening the double burden of women.*

While women contribute two-thirds of the hours worked in the world, they only earn about one-tenth of the world's income and own only about one percent of the world's property. Women's working conditions are more difficult than those of men, particularly because women's access to production resources is restricted. All countries should:

- Repeal all laws and practices preventing or restricting women from owning and administering productive resources;
- Recognize that women's access to technology and training has to be guaranteed in all aspects of the economy, not only in those occupations and tasks traditionally perceived as women's domain;
- Ensure that women have access to credit without collateral and improved access to markets in the agricultural and informal sector;
- Establish and enforce laws of equal pay for work of equal value;
- Measures to relieve women's workload—including improved domestic technology and better family planning services—should be a priority;
- All women should have access to safe water and fuel supply in or within reasonable distance of their homes;
- Child care should be a standard feature of workplaces on the same basis as other facilities;
- Child care and maternity leave should be on the same footing as health insurance and sick leave.

3. *Providing family planning.*

Giving women the ability to choose when and whether to have children has powerful posi-tive effects on their health, on the health of their children, and on their ability to involve themselves in the world outside the confines of the household. Providing family planning services may be one of the best ways of investing in women. It also has a profound effect on population growth. Countries should:

- Provide high quality services and a wide variety of family planning methods so that women can choose the one that best suits their needs;
- Provide appropriate and special family planning information and services for men, teenagers, unmarried and newly-married women—people who tend to be excluded from services which are usually combined with maternal and child health care;
- Provide full information about possible side effects of family planning so that women can make an informed choice;
- Ensure that women are consulted and involved at every level in the organization of family planning services, so that services are provided by appropriate staff in appropriate places at appropriate times;
- Ensure that prevention and treatment of infertility is an effective part of maternal and child health and family planning services;
- Include information, education, and communication and counseling about AIDS as an integral part of family planning services and promote the use of condoms in AIDS prevention.

4. *Improving the health of women.*

The most dangerous time for both a mother and her baby are usually the weeks surrounding birth. High infant deaths have serious effects on women's sense of security, and dangerous labor—if it does not result in a mother's death—can cause much long-term suffering and disability. Countries should:

- Train traditional birth attendants in hygiene; in promoting the benefits of birth spacing; in ensuring "at risk" births take place in a clinic setting;

- Concentrate interventions particularly on women who have lost two babies;

- Provide supplementary food for malnourished mothers—especially young teenage mothers—to help reduce the incidence of low birth weight babies to fewer than 10 percent of live births by the year 2000;

- Monitor nutrition of pre-school children—with separate norms of boys and girls—and ensure that at least 90 percent of children have a weight for age corresponding to international reference norms;

- Educate parents about the need to care for their daughters equally with their sons;

- Train women to assume supervisory and decision-making roles in the health sector.

5. *Expanding education.*

Educating girls gives them some of the basic skills and confidence to begin taking control of their lives, and opens up opportunities for them in the world outside the home. Education is perhaps the strongest variable affecting the status of women. Countries should:

- Expand girls' enrollment in school and their retention in the school system by active recruitment, counseling of dropouts, and reducing school fees if necessary;

- Halt the practice of expelling pregnant teenagers from school and encourage them to continue their education before and after the birth;

- Include sex education, family planning, and family responsibility in school curricula for children before they reach the age of first sexual experience;

- Encourage both girls and boys to study the whole range of subjects;

- Establish a framework of appropriate policies and programs to bring about appropriate attitudinal and behavioral changes among both women and men.

6. *Equality of opportunity.*

Despite the Decade for Women and the recommendations of the International Conferences of 1975 and 1985, many declarations, and much rhetoric, women in many parts of the world and in many communities have still not reached equality in status with men. In many ways this is a reflection of lack of understanding of the issues and the pervasiveness of deep-seated attitudes and belief systems.

There is an urgent need to change the attitudes of decision makers and leaders in favor of equality of opportunity for women, and for ensuring commitment to this cause at the highest levels of society.

Commitment will be expressed by high visibility for issues of women and development, followed by formulation of a policy and strategy on women and development, with adequate resources for its implementation. Women must be an integral part of the process of developing such a policy and strategy.

A legal and attitudinal framework which provides a basis for equality of status is essential. All countries should:

- Ratify and implement the International Convention on the Elimination of All

Forms of Discrimination Against Women;

- Review the legal system to remove barriers to women's full participation in society and the family on an equal basis with men, and eliminate the legal basis for discrimination;
- Educate both men and women at all levels, starting in the school system, to accept the principle that women and men are equal in value and have equal rights in society and the family;
- Promote women's access to decision making and leadership positions in government and private sector and ensure women's involvement in design and implementation of programs affecting women.

Women, Children, and Population

The lives of 5.6 million children and 200,000 women could be saved each year if all the women who wanted to limit their families had access to family planning.

The Danger

Unwanted pregnancies are dangerous—both for mothers and children.

Mothers

Five hundred thousand women die of maternal causes a year. More than 200,000 of these could be saved if they were able to plan their families.

Children

Ten million children under the age of five die a year—more than half of these as a result of poor maternal health during pregnancy, unsafe delivery, or inadequate care after birth.

The Cost

To bring family planning to all women who want it would cost an extra $2 billion a year until the year 2000. This is less than the annual U.S. expenditure on tobacco advertising.

(This account is reprinted from *Popline,* September-October 1989, pp. 4 and 5.)

Technology at the Turning Point

by Riane Eisler

This article, based on an address by Riane Eisler to the General Assembly of the World Future Society at World View '84, held June 9–15, 1984, in Washington, D.C., has previously appeared in International Synergy *(June 1987).*

A Manifesto for Transformation

Cultural evolution is our synergistic interaction with technology. From the very beginning, our brains and hands have been basic tools, altering the world. In our time, when megatechnics shape our environment more than nature itself, we are at a critical branching: how we use technology will determine our future—and whether we even have one.

Ours is the century of cybernetic intelligence, of supersonic transportation, of instantaneous global communication, and for the first time giving us the power of total world destruction once attributed only to God—of nuclear energy. It is an age when the ancient Blade, magnified a millionfold by advanced technology, threatens all life on this Earth, a time when we face the end of all human technology—and all human hopes and aspirations. But it is also a time that could signal the beginning of a new era for technology and humanity.

This is a manifesto of hope and of realism, of pragmatics and of faith, based on the knowledge that we *can* through both ancient and modern technologies, deconstruct conventional realities, freeing ourselves to reconstruct our minds and our world.

Savior or Destroyer? Toward a New Epistemology for Technology

Some people see modern technology as savior: the ultimate solution for humanity's age-old woes. To others technology is destructive:

the antihuman archvillain of modern times. For Buckminster Fuller, technology was the means to a better life.[1] Through World Game and other devices, Fuller and his followers demonstrated that modern technologies could feed, clothe, and otherwise provide for all of humanity. In contrast, for Jacques Ellul, technology—the past uses of mechanics to build inhuman assembly lines, the present uses of electronics to deaden human sensibilities—was dehumanizing.[2] This too is the view of Helen Caldicott, who so forcefully documents the terrible dangers to us and to our planet from nuclear technology.[3]

But if both views are right—if technology is both villain and savior—what is the real, underlying problem? Could it be that the technology as savior or villain debate obscures the basic issues? Do the answers to our mounting global problems require a completely different approach?

The approach here proposed derives from a ten-year study of the development of human technology from its earliest prehistoric appearance.[4] It offers a new way of viewing—and consciously using—technology. By cutting through old dogmas and preconceptions about both human and technological evolution (which are inextricably intertwined), it also sheds new light on why we have now come to the brink of technological Armageddon—and how we may draw back before it is too late.

One outcome of this study has been a new epistemological framework for the analysis of technology: a new system of classification and valuation moving beyond the conventional distinction between "high" versus "low," "good" versus "bad," "labor-intensive" versus "capital-intensive" technologies.

The first aspect of the epistemological framework I propose is a new way of defining and understanding technology. In conventional usage, technology is equated with what, borrowing from Lewis Mumford,[5] we may call *technics:* human-made tools, ranging from the most primitive stone and wood artifacts to the most elaborate mechanical and electronic devices. Yet if we examine the matter closely, we find that technology is a significantly larger concept. It is *the use of both tools or technics and our bodies and minds to achieve human-defined goals.* In other words, technology is dynamic, a living process rather than an inanimate thing. It is a reflection of both positive and negative possibilities for humanity, a co-creation of our species with the elements of nature.

Human technology is, above all, *human.* It is the amplification and extension of integral human functions—of our hands' capacity to make tools (ranging from potter's wheels, hoes, and mill stones to industrial machinery and electronic robotics), our tongues' capacity to fashion language (now vastly expanded through radio, records, telephones, and television), our legs' capacity for transport (all the way from the horse-drawn carriage to such complex technics as automobiles and supersonic aircraft). Beyond that, technology is the product of our brains' unique capacity to image and create for ourselves functions *not* inherent in our genetic repertoire (such as our creation of airplanes that fly like birds or of solar technics that, like plants, process the rays of the sun into usable energy).

The second, even more important, change I propose for the study of technology takes us even further beyond the conventional approach. Rather than viewing technology as one big category into which we may toss everything from can openers to hydrogen bombs, it divides technology into *four basic categories defined by the ends to which they are directed.*

The first, most familiar and widely established, is the *technology of production.* This includes technologies such as farming, weaving, manufacturing, and construction. These may consist of the use of only our hands and minds.

Or they may be the extension of these functions, be it through our first stone and wood tools or through modern technics such as machines and computers. What distinguishes technologies of production is the fact that their primary purpose is to sustain and enhance human life.

A second type, less familiar to conventional thought, is the *technology of reproduction.* The most familiar technology here is the human capacity to give birth inherent in women's wombs. Also increasingly familiar are the technologies of reproductive planning or birth control. But today technologies of reproduction also include technologies for the replacement of bodily parts, like kidneys and hearts. And, although this is a matter of enormous controversy, some day they may include technics for creating life in laboratories.

The third type of technology is the *technology of actualization.* Also age old, but not commonly thought of in this way, this encompasses human technologies such as art and education, which are integral to human society and socialization. Although often distorted into means for social and personal control, the purpose of these technologies is the actualization of our species' unique potentials. Examples are not only personal technologies, such as meditation for spiritual growth, biofeedback for self-healing, and other uses of our minds' still largely untapped capacities for the realization of our human growth potentials. Technologies of actualization are also social technologies such as public education, peace conferences, representative politics, equitable economics, democratic families, and other human inventions for the construction of the kind of society that can facilitate, rather than impede, the realization of our highest human potentials: what I call a partnership rather than a dominator model of social organization.

Finally, there is a fourth type of technology that is wholly different from the first three. This is the *technology of destruction.* The purpose of this type of technology is not to create, but to destroy and dominate. Technologies of destruction include all the technics of terror, beginning with the sharp blade of the ancient warrior, now culminating with the global threat of nuclear warheads. But they also include technologies inherent in our bodies, such as muscular strength, which can be used either as a technology of production, or—as we have seen all too vividly in the bloody centuries of recorded history—as a technology to rob others of their material possessions, as well as to conquer, pillage, and exert personal and/or social control.

In sum, the new epistemological framework here proposed not only divides technology into four basic categories; by focusing on *ends* rather than *means,* it makes it possible to make a functional distinction between positive and negative types of technologies. Simplifying what otherwise appear to be unmanageable complexities, this new view (which for reasons that will become apparent I call the *partnership/dominator* schema) offers a new method (and grounds) for the analysis of technology: one that makes it possible to ask more precise, practical, and productive questions. It takes us directly to the relationship between technology and society, delineating what we need to know about modern technology and how we can apply this knowledge to solve our mounting global problems.

Simply stating this system of classification makes it evident that it is not technology that is the problem. Rather, it is our *human choices* of life-destroying versus life-enhancing technologies. Even more precisely, although as we have seen technologies of production, reproduction, and actualization can be distorted and misused for domination, the major problem of our time is our choice of the technologies of destruction over the technologies that in active partnership with nature enable us to create and sustain human culture and human life.

But again, this recognition of the factor of human choice underlying our present techno-logical crises is only the surface of a much larger picture. The real question is *what determines these choices*. For human choices, as the social sciences have amply demonstrated, are not made in a vacuum. They are heavily influenced by our socialization, which in turn is a function of our social and economic organization.

So the basic questions for our technology and our future are these: What kind of social organization will give technologies of production, reproduction, and actualization priority? Conversely, what kind of social organization forces the world, century after century, to invest so many millions of lives and billions of dollars in the technologies of destruction?

The Evolution of Technology

A good starting point toward answers to these questions is provided by our earliest beginnings as humans, when the development of our uniquely human brain and erect posture first made it possible for women and men to use their hands and minds to make and use tools. If we look at the entire spectrum of human history from this early perspective, some startling answers emerge.

First, as Mary and Richard Leakey as well as other experts on our earliest fossil remains have stressed time and again, contrary to the ideas popularized by books like *The Naked Ape* and *The Territorial Imperative,* we were not, as the movie *2001* portrayed, shaggy humanoids who discovered the beauty and power of technology by beating each other to death with big bones.[6] As works such as those of Nancy Tanner, Adrienne Zihlman, and Jane Lancaster propose, rather than relating to killing, the biological and technological developments that make us uniquely human most probably related to sharing: to the shift from foraging (or eating as one goes) to gathering and carrying food so it could be both shared and stored.[7]

Our first artifacts were *not* technologies of destruction. Developed long before large game

215

was hunted and warfare began, they were technologies of production: containers for carrying, storing, and also sharing food with other members of the troop and for carrying babies, as well as for softening food for infants to eat. Correspondingly, our first social bonds were not the bonds between men required to kill. The basic social bond, making possible the emergence of the traits that make our species unique (and to this day holding human society together) is the bonding between mothers and children that is required if human offspring (with the exceptionally long maturation period required for our full physical and mental development) are to survive.

Moreover, as we move from proto-history into prehistory, the most striking thing about the Paleolithic era is the enormous emphasis on technologies of *actualization*. Already in the nineteenth century, scholars were discovering the extraordinary cave paintings of the Paleolithic. They were also finding hundreds of what they then called Venus figurines—which are *not,* as formerly asserted, manifestations of male eroticism, ancient counterparts of *Playboy* centerfolds. Rather, as modern archeologists have proven, these full-bodied, often pregnant, highly stylized female carvings were the earliest anthropomorphic religious images: representations of the deity in human form. They were artistic imaginings of the life-giving and sustaining powers of the universe: the precursors of the Mother Goddess figurines so ubiquitous in the Neolithic and Bronze Age eras.[8]

Once again in dramatic contradiction to what we have been taught, new archeological findings show that the Neolithic or agrarian revolution did *not* usher in warfare, slavery, and the subjugation of women. In fact, it is the fascinating, new, but as yet little known, data from the Neolithic that most illuminate the early partnership rather than dominator history of technology. For these finds—by archeologists like James Mellaart of the British Institute of Archeology and Marija Gimbutas of UCLA,

who are part of a veritable revolution in archeology—offer us the most extensive evidence showing that the social emphasis on technologies of destruction, which fills most of what we have until recently known of our history, is *not* inevitable.

Thanks to new scientific dating methods, we now know of Neolithic societies that lasted for many thousands of years, which often had standards of living higher than those we see today in some of the poorer nations of our world. It is in these societies (which as Mellaart writes were the true cradles of civilization, arising thousands of years before Sumer) that we find the first flowering of all the technologies on which civilization is based. We see here not only the domestication of plants and animals required to produce the surpluses that ensure a sustained food supply. We also find other sophisticated technologies of production, such as advanced stone and metal toolmaking, great strides in the making of clothing, pottery, rugs, and jewelry, and highly developed construction technologies, including even town planning. Above all, what we find is an emphasis on technologies of actualization, evidenced by a rich, and highly revealing, artistic tradition.[9]

This artistic tradition is hopeful because of the absence of something that fills so much of the art of later cultures, including our own: the glorification of warriors and war. Back in Neolithic times of surprising levels of civilization there is a remarkable lack of images of armed warriors, scenes of battles, and fierce chieftains, or anything like the ubiquitous scenes of aggrandized kings taking back prisoners in chains characteristic of later art. Moreover, in the archeological remains of these societies—in contrast to what came later—there is a general absence of fortifications. In short, while in knives, axes, scythes, and spears (regularly used for farming and hunting) they clearly had technics that could be used for destruction, there are no signs that such technics were, as in our time, routinely used in wars.[10]

In these Neolithic (and later also Chalcolithic and Bronze Age) societies, as both Mellaart and Gimbutas stress, the social organization was basically equalitarian. Although there were differences in status and in wealth, these were not marked. Most notably—contrary to the old stereotypes of "divinely ordained" or "natural" male supremacy—there were here women priestesses, women craftspeople, and (to us most surprising) the supreme deity was conceptualized as female rather than male: all specific indications that women were *not* subordinate to men.[11]

In the most basic technological terms—of human functions as the fundamental human technologies—these were societies where men did not use greater size and musculature as technologies of destruction. They did not routinely conquer one another to create systems of a few masters with many slaves or those only slightly better off than slaves. This is not to say that these were ideal societies or that there was here no violence. But because here the primary principle of social organization seems to have been our *linking* by mutual trust and caring, rather than our *ranking* imposed by force, these were societies which did *not* give highest value to technologies of destruction.

But, as Mellaart and Gimbutas record, about five thousand years ago this original direction in the mainstream of western cultural evolution was violently interrupted by people, who, as Gimbutas writes, "worshiped the lethal power of the blade."[12] In western prehistory (which is what we have been concentrating on, as this is where we have the most archeological excavations), these were a pastoral people scholars call Indo-Europeans, who came down from the arid steppes of the northeast. Theirs were societies in which the use of *force* for *ranking* (of men over women and of a strongman elite over other men) was the primary principle of social organization. And here—as we still do today, having inherited *their* values and *their* violent social organization—the highest priority was given to technologies of destruction. Just as in modern times, the highest honor was thus accorded to the "noble warrior."

Even when, after millennia of chaos and devastation, these barbarian invaders began to settle down, absorbing some of the more civilized ways of the peoples they conquered—when our social and technological development resumed—these conquerors saw to it that it was in a very different direction from what it had been originally. And this direction—this course no longer guided by the Chalice, the ancient vessel of physical regeneration and spiritual illumination, but by the lethal Blade—is still with us today.

The Invisibility of the Obvious

Until their rediscovery by modern archeology, we had no hard evidence of prehistoric societies with different social and technological priorities. But we *did* know about them. For folk memories about them survived in myths and legends: legends we are all, in fact, extremely familiar with.

Every one of us is familiar with the biblical story of a more innocent time when humanity lived in a garden (as Neolithic people did because, as the first farmers, they planted the first gardens on this earth). We also know this was a time *before* woman was (as the biblical myth has it) condemned by a male god to be subservient to man. Moreover, we know that such legends are also found in other ancient works. One example is the Chinese *Tao Te Ching,* where we read of a more peaceful and harmonious time before the yin or feminine principle was subservient to the yang or male principle.[13] Another is the work of the Greek poet Hesiod, who wrote of an earlier and nobler "golden race," who also lived in a garden and did not make war.[14]

One of the best-known stories of a lost ancient civilization is the legend of Atlantis. This tale of a rich and fabulous prehistoric civiliza-

217

tion is now believed by scholars to be a garbled folk memory not of a sunken continent but of a remarkable Bronze Age civilization that once flourished in the Mediterranean. This was the civilization rediscovered at the turn of the twentieth century in Crete and surrounding islands, where circa 1400 B.C.E. severe earthquakes in fact sank large masses of land into the sea.[15]

The amazingly advanced civilization of Minoan Crete has now been scientifically excavated, revealing its particular significance for our study of the history of technology. For if we closely look at the archeological finds from Crete, we see that this was the one place where a way of structuring human relations based on linking rather than ranking survived into recorded or historical times.

In Crete remarkably "modern" advances in technologies of production were used to build the first viaducts, the first paved roads, and even the first indoor plumbing in Europe. Here technologies of actualization flourished into an uniquely beautiful and rich art. And here the supreme power was still viewed as the life-sustaining and enhancing power of the "feminine" Chalice rather than the death-wielding power of the "masculine" Blade. As archeologist Nicolas Platon, former Superintendent of Antiquities in Crete and Director of the Acropolis Museum, writes: "The whole of life was pervaded by an ardent faith in the goddess Nature, the source of all creation and harmony." Most significantly from a systems perspective is that in this society—where, as Platon writes, "the important part played by women is discernible in every sphere," there was also, in Platon's words, "a love of peace, a horror of tyranny, and a respect for the law."[16]

In our time, when a love of peace, a horror of tyranny, and a respect for the law are often derided as impossible utopian dreams, this kind of information is of far more than academic interest. *It demonstrates something that, while still generally ignored, is obvious in systems terms. This is that the way we structure the most fundamental of all human relations—that between the female and male halves of humanity—profoundly affects the totality of a social system, including its technological direction.*

What these archeological data document is that a social system in which the larger and stronger male half of humanity dominates the female half—and to maintain this dominance is systematically taught to equate masculinity with conquest and aggression—will in its social priorities emphasize technologies of destruction. For in such a *dominator* society human rankings—beginning with the ranking of male over female—are ultimately backed up by force or the threat of force. In contrast is the social system where the female and male halves are valued equally; where, beginning with the most fundamental difference between male and female, diversity is *not* equated with inferiority or superiority. In such systems, "feminine" values such as caring, compassion, and non-violence can operationally be given social priority. Consequently, in these *partnership* societies, technologies to sustain and enhance life—rather than technologies to dominate and destroy—can have precedence.

The link between gender-dominance and an emphasis on technologies of destruction that emerges from the new archeology is further verified by the new anthropology—particularly in recent anthropological studies of warfare. For example, in 1976, anthropologists Divale and Harris found a significant correlation between the extent to which a tribe engaged in warfare and the degree to which it was structured on sexual inequality.[17] A 1978 study by Arkin and Dobrofsky extensively documents how the stereotype of the he-man (the conquest-oriented male) and male dominance over women is central to the way the military teaches soldiers to use technologies of destruction in war.[18] Similarly, using a randomly selected sample of preindustrial cultures, McConahay and McConahay in 1977 found a statistically significant relationship between violence and rigid male-female stereotypes. They found that rigidly male-dominant societies (with correspondingly rigid stereotypes of "masculinity" and "femininity") were characteristically more violent. Specifically, this violence was institutionalized—i.e., integrated into daily life through institutions and socially condoned—through punitive observed violence in child rearing, rape, wife beating, blood feuds, and violence against other groups in the form of raids and wars.[19]

Indeed, if we look at our own time, we see that warlike regimes like those of the Ayatollah Khomeini in Iran and the Reagan administration in the U.S. show the same general systems correlations between an emphasis on technologies of destruction and domination and rigid stereotypes of dominant "masculinity" and subdominant "femininity." One of the slogans of the Reagan administration, which systematically dismantled policies aimed at ending sex-based discrimination, was the return of women to their "traditional place." This same administration pushed for the highest budget for technologies of destruction the world has ever seen. And completing the three-way configuration that characterizes dominator systems (the interlinking of male dominance, institutionalized male violence, and a generally hierarchic and authoritarian social organization), this was the same administration that reinstituted economic policies openly favoring those on top (with those on bottom to get only what "trickles down") while at the same time both overtly and covertly funding a wide range of violent and authoritarian regimes.

As the "Irangate" scandal revealed, among these regimes was that of the most notorious instigator of world terrorism: the misogynistic, repressive, and warlike Ayatollah Khomeini of Iran. This was the same Khomeini who was originally expelled from Iran for leading a bloody three-day riot protesting laws that gave women somewhat more equality, who—following the systems link between male supremacy and the valuing of technologies of destruction

above all others—mounted a "holy war" against Iraq, incited the violent kidnapping of American hostages, and ordered the public executions of anyone who did not strictly obey his orders. These executions, most significantly, included Baha'i women (among them Iran's first woman concert pianist, a former television executive, and two teenage college students) hanged for the "crime" of clinging to a faith which proclaims the equality of women and men.[20]

In sum, despite the great cultural, economic, and religious differences of the United States and Iran, what we have today in America behind the benign, grinning facade of a "nice-guy" President, are actually the very same systems dynamics that drive the horror of the Khomeini regime in Iran. Only here they are less extreme and more subtle—but because of our size and influence just as dangerous to the world.

Technology and Transformation

How are we to break free from this dominator model of society that has throughout the blood-stained centuries of recorded history used violence to maintain its hold?

The history we have been taught has focused on the use of technologies of destruction. It has been the history of dominator systems: of the bloody rise and fall of empires, of wars, of violence. But there is another side of history: the periodic thrust toward the partnership model of society.

If we look at the systems correlations between rigid male dominance, warfare, and authoritarian repression in the context of the kinds of data I have briefly summarized, we see that beneath the complexities of technology and human history are striking patterns. We see that it is not so strange that societies that view the two basic human types—females and males—primarily in terms of ranking one above the other should also see all of humanity in the same way. And we also see why and how societies where boys with toys and men with guns are systematically taught to equate masculinity with domination, and thus to value *themselves* as technologies of destruction—as "noble warriors"—must also obsessively build, buy, and ultimately use, ever more "advanced" weapons.

If we reexamine human society from a truly holistic perspective, taking into account both our history and our prehistory and both the female and male halves of our species, it is also possible to see that our mounting global problems are indeed not solvable under a dominator system—*for they are the consequences of a dominator model of society at our level of technological development*. Hence, there is in our time an irreconcilable conflict between the requirements for *dominator* systems survival and *human* systems survival.

The recognition, still largely unconscious but here and there forthrightly articulated, that the dominator system is approaching its logical end—and with it *our* end—is what lies behind the unprecedented global movement toward a partnership society. It is this recognition that lies behind the mounting rejection of the "hard" stereotypically labeled "masculine" values symbolized by the Blade. And it is what fuels the growing impetus toward reinstating to social governance such "softer" values as empathy, sensitivity, and compassion—the stereotypically labeled "feminine" values symbolized by the Chalice.

In sum, what ultimately lies behind such seemingly unconnected modern movements as the peace, feminist, and ecology movements is the survival impulse of our species. And it is also this survival drive that lies behind the great modern battle over technology; including the fact that women are today demanding an end to men's exclusive control over all the primary technologies, especially the technologies of reproduction inherent in women's own bodies.

The real issue, integrally related to the great contemporary debate of technology as savior or villain, is that in our high technology age,

a dominator society is fundamentally maladaptive, threatening not only our species, but all life forms on this planet. For how can the population explosion be arrested as long as women are denied access to birth control technologies, as long as they themselves continue to be viewed primarily as technologies for reproduction? How can environmental pollution and degradation be arrested as long as men continue to identify with the "manly" conquest of nature rather than the "women's work" of environmental housekeeping? Most critically, how can we survive in a world still ruled by the Blade at a time when we have the ultimate technologies of destruction: the technologies for ending all life.

This leads directly to the final, and practically speaking most critical, statement in this manifesto: the fact that the transformation from a dominator to a partnership system can*not* be effected through violence. As the failure of modern progressive revolutions amply demonstrates, technologies of destruction in fact only replace one dominator system with another. How then can this transformation be effected? What technologies can successfully be used?

A central theme of *The Chalice and the Blade* is the transformative power of communication. This book shows not only how the original partnership direction of cultural evolution over many thousands of peaceful and prosperous years before war and the war of the sexes was violently interrupted; it also shows how the imposition of a dominator system was accomplished in the long term, not only by the sword, but by the pen. For the imposition and maintenance of a dominator society would have been impossible in the long run without a transformation of human consciousness: a reprogramming of the human mind to view men's use of force or the threat of force to dominate or destroy as "divinely ordained," "natural," and, above all else, "manly."[21]

The priests (who were often also the scribes) of antiquity served the ruling castes. It was their job to use the media of communication to manufacture and disseminate a dominator world view. Backed up by armed might, these men exercised complete and monolithic control over all media. Deviations from the officially sanctioned world view were punishable by death through torture—and presumably even after death and for all eternity by vengeful gods. Thus, the informatics of domination were implanted in the deepest recesses of our collective unconscious, as hallowed and immutable truths.

Intermittently, with periodic shifts toward a partnership model, this monolithic thought control weakened; a process greatly accelerated in modern times by technologies of mass communication such as the printing press and later film, radio, and television. The old pyramidal universe—where a male god (and his earthly representatives, the kings and high priests of old) rules over all men, who in turn rule over women, children, and the rest of nature—was challenged in bits and pieces by progressive modern ideologies such as republicanism, socialism, and feminism.

But until now there has been no integrated ideology to replace the old, no informatics of partnership to replace the informatics of domination.[22] So the mass media are still used to reinflame the old in-group versus out-group fears and prejudices (as they are today under the guise of morality by both Moslem and Christian fundamentalists) to justify man's inhumanity to man—and woman. In films like *Rambo,* the old message that "real men" prove they are right by violence is reidealized. And on television, actor-politicians continue to spread disinformation at the same time that the most violent mass "entertainment" since the days of the Roman Empire deadens our capacity for empathy.

These are the mind-enslaving uses of modern communication technologies in a dominator society—already foreshadowed in the fiction of George Orwell's *1984* and the facts of modern totalitarians and would-be totalitarians

from both Right and Left. But there is also the other side: the unprecedented potential of modern mass media as instruments of transformation, as technologies to free our minds, to reawaken our consciousness, to help us regain our empathy—our sense of connection with other humans and nature.[23]

Today, for the first time in all of history, we have technologies of communication of such sweep and power that they can in a matter of seconds beam world-changing social-symbolic constructions into every corner of our globe. At a time when one more war could be our last, these modern mass media provide the technological capacity to exponentially accelerate the major transformation in human consciousness that can take us from a dominator to a partnership mentality.

Figuratively and literally, communication *is* society and society *is* communication. Media are the technologies of communication, transmuting myth into reality and reality into myth, shaping our consciousness and in turn shaped by it.

The most urgent issue of our time is how we can rapidly move the partnership technologies—the technologies of production, reproduction, and actualization symbolized by the Chalice—*up,* and the dominator technologies of destruction symbolized by the Blade *down,* on our scale of values. Our incredibly powerful mass media are the *nonviolent* technologies that can help us resume our stunted cultural evolution. The conscious, creative, and concerted use of such technics as transnational television, intercontinental telecommunications, and communications satellites—which can move messages that once took days, months, and even years with the speed of light—can effectively reverse the process that in our prehistory took millennia, redirecting us from a world of chronic wars and violence to one of partnership and peace.

Our advanced communication technologies provide the way, but do we have the *will*?

As one broadcaster of vision, Ted Turner, writes, will we use our technology to beam death rays at each other, or to beam messages of hope?[24] Will we use our technologies of communication as conveyors of the informatics of domination or partnership?

A long time ago, in 1848, a man and a woman proclaimed their manifestos. The man's is very well known: Karl Marx's manifesto urging the workers of the world to recognize their essential unity.[25] The woman's manifesto is not well known: Elizabeth Cady Stanton's urging of the women of the world to recognize their essential unity.[26]

This manifesto urges *all* of humanity to recognize our essential unity: our kinship with one another, with nature, and at the same time, our unique place in nature as co-creators of our own evolution. As stated, it is a manifesto of hope and of realism, of pragmatics and of faith, based on the knowledge that we *can,* through both ancient and modern partnership technologies, deconstruct conventional realities, freeing ourselves to reconstruct our minds and our world.

Since the time of Karl Marx and Elizabeth Cady Stanton there have been other manifestos. Some of these, like Filippo Marinetti's "Futurist Manifesto" of 1909, promised a very different kind of unity: the enforced unity of a dominator future, a world of "Ideas that kill! Contempt for women!"[27] This too was the violent, totalitarian world heralded in that most famous of all modern dominator manifestos: Hitler's *Mein Kampf.* Such statements, reglorifying war and the "masculinity" of warriors, and their spread through the mass media of the time, preceded the outbreak of both World Wars I and II. As conveyors of the informatics of domination, they asserted their ultimate faith in the Blade: the "revolutionary" power of megadeath technics of destruction and domination.

This is a manifesto not of revolution but of *transformation*. Its ultimate faith is in life, not death. Inspired not by the Blade, but by the Chalice—the ancient symbol of life-enhancing and transformative power—it is a statement of faith in the creative and illuminating power of our highest aspirations: our age-old striving for truth, beauty, and justice. Above all, it is a statement of faith and hope in *us,* in our technological power as humans to deconstruct the myths of dominator reality and reconstruct ourselves and this planet into the new synergisms suitable for a world of partnership and peace.

Notes

1. See, e.g., R. Buckminster Fuller, *Operating Manual for Spaceship Earth* (New York: Pocket Book, 1970).

2. Jacques Ellul, *The Technological Society* (New York: Knopf, 1964).

3. Helen Caldicott, *Nuclear Madness* (New York: Bantam Books, 1980). Other important books on technology and its misuses are Hazel Henderson's *The Politics of the Solar Age* (Garden City, New York: Anchor Press, 1981), E. F. Schumacher's *Small Is Beautiful* (New York: Harper & Row, 1973), and *Smothered by Invention: Technology in Women's Lives,* Wendy Faulkner and Erik Arnold, eds. (London: Pluto Press, 1985).

4. The first book reporting findings from this study is Riane Eisler, *The Chalice and the Blade: Our History, Our Future* (San Francisco: Harper & Row, 1987).

5. Lewis Mumford, *The Myth of the Machine: Technics and Human Development* (New York: Harcourt, Brace & World, 1966).

6. For some refutations of the idea popularized by books such as Desmond Morris's *The Naked Ape* (New York: McGraw-Hill, 1967) and Robert Ardrey's *African Genesis* (New York: Atheneum, 1966) that "man is a born killer," see Richard Leakey and Roger Lewis, *People of the Lake* (New York: Anchor/Doubleday, 1978), Ashley Montagu, *The Nature of Human Aggression* (New York: Oxford University Press, 1976) and Ashley Montagu (ed.) *Sociobiology Examined* (New York: Oxford University Press, 1980).

7. Nancy Tanner, *On Becoming Human* (Boston: Cambridge University Press, 1981), Adrienne Zihlman, *Motherhood in Transition: From Ape to Human*, in Warren Miller and Lucille Newman (eds.), *The First Child and Family Formation* (Chapel Hill, N.C.: Carolina Population Center, 1978), Jane Lancaster, *Carrying and Sharing in Human Evolution, Human Nature* 1, 2, February 1978, 82–89.

8. As British archeologist James Mellaart writes, as long as Paleolithic art was viewed as nothing more than "an expression of hunting magic" there was little hope the link between these figures and the Great Goddess later worshiped in the Near East could be established (James Mellaart, *Catal Huyuk* [New York: McGraw-Hill, 1967], p. 23). For an excellent critique of the astonishing blindness of many scholars to the mythic significance of the Paleolithic female imagery, see Marija Gimbutas, *The Image of Woman in Prehistoric Art, The Quarterly Review of Archeology*, December 1981, pp. 6–9.

9. For some fascinating discussions and illustrations of Neolithic life and art, see Marija Gimbutas, *The Goddesses and Gods of Old Europe, 7000–3500 B.C.* (Berkeley and Los Angeles: University of California Press, 1982) and James Mellaart, *The Neolithic of the Near East* (New York: Scribner, 1975).

10. Marija Gimbutas, *The Beginning of the Bronze Age in Europe and the Indo-Europeans: 3500–2500 B.C., Journal of Indo-European Studies* 1 (1973) provides a vivid account of the early history of metallurgy. Originally used by the old European cultures for making tools, ritual vessels, and jewelry (in other words, technologies of production and actualization) metals were in the hands of their Indo-European invaders converted into a means for making weapons. See also note 9.

11. See note 9.

12. Marija Gimbutas, *The First Wave of Eurasian Steppe Pastoralists into Copper Age Europe, Journal of Indo-European Studies* no. 5 (Winter 1977), p. 281.

13. R. B. Blakney, ed. and trans., *The Way of Life: Tao Te Ching* (New York: Mentor, 1955).

14. Hesiod, *Works and Days,* quoted in John Mansley Robinson, *An Introduction to Early Greek Philosophy* (Boston: Houghton Mifflin, 1968), pp. 12–13.

15. One of the first scholars to advance this theory was Spyridon Marinatos, in *The Volcanic Destruction of Minoan Crete, Antiquity* no. 13 (1939), pp. 425–39. See also Nikolas Platon, *Crete* (Geneva: Nagel Publishers, 1966), p. 69. Platon stresses that to explain the "Greek miracle" we must look to pre-Hellenic tradition. Another scholar who focuses on the Minoan roots of ancient Greece is Jacquetta Hawkes in *Dawn of the Gods: Minoan and Mycenaean Origins of Greece* (New York: Random House, 1968).

16. Nikolas Platon, *Crete* (Geneva: Nagel Publishers, 1966), p. 161.

17. William Divale and Marvin Harris, "Population, Warfare and the Male Supremacist Complex," *American Anthropologist* 78 (1976): 521–38.

18. William Arkin and Lynne Dobrofsky, "Military Socialization and Masculinity," *Journal of Social Issues* 24 (1978): 151–168.

19. Shirley McConahay and John McConahay, "Sexual Permissiveness, Sex Role Rigidity, and Violence Across Cultures," *Journal of Social Issues* no. 33, (1977): 134–143.

20. *Women's International Network News* no. 9 (Autumn 1983): 42. For a discussion of the relationship between the suppression of liberty and the suppression of women, see Riane Eisler, "Human Rights: Toward an Integrated Theory for Action," in *Feminist Issues* Vol. 7, No. 1, Spring 1987 and *The Human Rights Quarterly* Vol. 9, No. 3, August 1987.

21. Riane Eisler, *The Chalice and the Blade: Our History, Our Future* (San Francisco: Harper & Row, 1987). The deadening of the human capacity for empathy, particularly in the socialization of males, is integral to male-dominant systems. This is related not only to the priority such systems give to technologies of destruction but also to irresponsible and uncaring applications of technology, a subject beyond the scope of this paper. Examples are the lack of safety protections in industry and mining that in the nineteenth century led to many unnecessary deaths, and more recently the nuclear accidents of Three Mile Island and Chernobyl.

22. I am indebted to Donna Haraway for the term "informatics of domination" which is here contrasted to what I call the "informatics of partnership."

23. See, e.g., Allyn B. Brodsky and David Dunn, *Art, Science, and Evolution, IS Journal #3* (December 1986). Among the more articulate modern social critics of destructive uses of technologies of communication are Theodore Roszak, Ivan Illich, and Morris Berman. For an important recent work pointing out that the issue is not so much one of technology but of politics, see Samson B. Knoll, "The Responsibility of Knowledge: Humanistic Perspectives in Information Management," in Eric H. Boehm and Michael K. Buckland, eds., *Education for Information Management: Directions for the Future* (Santa Barbara: International Academy at Santa Barbara, 1983). For a report on one of the first and largest studies showing the harmful effects of television violence on adult behavior—and also how prosocial behavior is encouraged by prosocial programs, see David Loye, "Television Effects: It's Not All Bad News," *Psychology Today,* May 1978 and David Loye, Roderic Gorney, and Gary Steele, "Effects of Television: An Experimental Field Study," *Journal of Communications,* Vol. 27, 1977, pp. 206–16.

24. Ted Turner, quoted in 1987 mailing from Better World Society, Washington, D.C.

25. Karl Marx and Friedrich Engels, *Manifesto of the Communist Party,* in *The Marx and Engels Reader,* second edition, Robert C. Tucker, ed. (New York: Norton, 1978), pp. 469–501.

26. Elizabeth Cady Stanton, *Address Delivered at Seneca Falls,* July 19, 1848, reprinted in Ellen Carol DuBois, ed., *Elizabeth Cady Stanton/Susan B. Anthony: Correspondence, Writings, Speeches* (New York: Schocken Books, 1981).

27. Filippo Marinetti's Futurist Manifesto quoted in Theodore Roszak, *The Hard and the Soft: The Force of Feminism in Modern Times,* in Betty and Theodore Roszak, eds., *Masculine/Feminine* (New York: Harper & Row, 1969), p. 91.

ABOUT THE CHALICE AND THE BLADE

Hailed by Princeton anthropologist Ashley Montagu as "the most important book since Darwin's *Origin of Species*," *The Chalice and the Blade* has not only had a remarkable publishing history, it has also launched a global movement.

Within two years after its publication by Harper & Row in 1987, it had gone into fifteen printings and been published or acquired for publication in French, German, Greek, Italian, Japanese, Finnish, Portuguese, and Spanish.

The Chalice and the Blade has also

- inspired the spontaneous formation of study groups worldwide,
- been adopted as a text in courses on peace studies, philosophy, sociology, Western history, women's studies, and other disciplines in the humanities and social sciences,
- been widely used by therapists who are recommending it to patients and find it catalytic for healing by business people who have successfully applied its ideas; and by thousands of women and men who report it has changed their lives,
- led to the formation of a new international organization, the Center for Partnership Studies, and Centers for Partnership Education in regions throughout the United States dedicated to turning the book's ideas into action.

Here is a selection of quotes that provides a good, quick sense of the book and its significance, as well as a reprint of a review by Helen Knode that originally appeared in *L.A. Weekly*.

"Apart from Darwin's *Origin of Species*, no book has impressed me as profoundly as *The Chalice and the Blade*."—Ashley Montagu, Princeton anthropologist

"Everyone . . . should have the opportunity to read it."—*Chicago Tribune*

". . . fascinating reading."—*Booklist*

"The greatest murder mystery and cover-up of all time."—*New Age Journal*

". . . a blueprint for a better future . . . validates a belief in humanity's capacity for benevolence and cooperation."—*San Francisco Chronicle*

". . . clears up many historical mysteries . . . provides foundations upon which to build a more humanistic world."—*The Humanist*

". . . one of the most important books of the year."—*Minneapolis Star & Tribune*

". . . an imaginative and persuasive work." —*Library Journal*

". . . an ambitious new synthesis . . . rigorous research . . . traces the unseen forces that shape human culture."—*Los Angeles Times*

". . . casts new light on all major problems . . . brings new clarity to the entire man-woman question . . . a major contribution."—Jean Baker Miller, M.D., director Stone Center, Wellesley College

". . . both scholarly and passionate . . . essential reading."—Fritjof Capra, physicist

"Some books are revelations, they open the spirit to unimaginable possibilities. *The Chalice and the Blade* is one of those magnificent key books. . . . —Isabel Allende, author of *The House of the Spirits*.

". . . perhaps a key to our survival . . . an enormous achievement."—Daniel Ellsberg, former Pentagon advisor

". . . a daring journey from pole to pole of human existence."—Charles Tilly, professor of history, New School for Social Research

"A gem . . . a rare combination of poetic expression and sober substance."—Jessie Bernard, professor of sociology

". . . a notable application of science to the growth and survival of human understanding."—Marija Gimbutas, professor of archeology, UCLA

". . . shows how our political and economic systems may attain a new balance."—Hazel Henderson, futurist

". . . a very important picture of human evolution."—Nikolas Platon, former director, Acropolis Museum, Athens

". . . required reading for anyone who is concerned about our destiny on Earth."—Ervin Laszlo, former director of research, United Nations

". . . an exciting and germinal work."—Robert Jungk, winner 1986 Alternative Nobel Peace Prize

". . . a catalytic and pioneering example of general evolution theory at work."—Ralph Abraham, professor, UCSC

"A groundbreaking book . . . brilliant research . . . will greatly influence and change our lives."—*Women's International Network News*

". . . as important, perhaps more important, than the unearthing of Troy or the deciphering of cuneiform."—Bruce Wilshire, professor of philosophy, Rutgers University

Apocalypse No:
A Review of
The Chalice and the Blade

by Helen Knode

The following book review excerpts are reprinted from L.A. Weekly, *June 19–25, 1987.*

The Chalice and the Blade may be the most significant work published in all our lifetimes. Princeton anthropologist Ashley Montagu calls it "the most important book since Darwin's *Origin of Species*." Start reading it; it doesn't appear to be earth-shattering. Futurist/feminist/international legal expert Riane Eisler has a very unhurried, straightforward manner of communicating her thoughts. No portentousness, no scary visions of hell, no big claims about her mission to save humankind. Yet motivating *The Chalice and the Blade* are some profoundly radical questions:

"Why do we hunt and persecute each other?" Eisler asks in the introduction to her book. "Why is our world so full of man's infamous inhumanity to man—and to woman? How can human beings be so brutal to their own kind? What is it that chronically tilts us toward cruelty rather than kindness, toward war rather than peace, toward destruction rather then actualization?"

In these four innocent-seeming questions, Eisler challenges a whole range of deeply ingrained assumptions: that human beings are each other's mortal enemies, that competitiveness between people is natural, and that the biological difference between men and women dictates women's subordinate status. (In other words, she's challenging the social-scientist/philosopher she's compared to, Darwin.) She's also ultimately asking the question: Do we have to destroy our species and the planet in a nuclear war?

Eisler's answers are as radical, and as radically simple, as her questions: No, humans don't have to hate and oppress each other. No, women are not naturally inferior to men. No, deadly competitiveness is not intrinsic to human nature. And no, we don't have to die in a great ball of fire. In the end, *The Chalice and the Blade* offers hope.

If Eisler presented no evidence for her claims, however comforting they might be, she'd just be another run-of-the-mill utopian, a dreamy New Ager on the loose. But she has mustered, organized, and interpreted a staggering amount of proof that for 15,000 years of human history, people lived in relative peace, women were not an underclass, and society was not rigidly stratified with the rich at the top, the poor at the bottom. In addition, contrary to the notion that only competition produces human progress, Eisler shows how the societies of the Neolithic age (from approximately 6000 B.C.) developed all the basic tools and technologies that we use today– agriculture, metallurgy, architecture, urban planning, writing, weaving, sanitation. These peoples also worshiped not a cruel God or an array of capricious, vengeful gods, but the Great Goddess, symbol of fertility, life, regeneration, and the bounty of the earth.

Eisler traces the evolution of these ancient cultures—as well as she can, given the incompleteness of the record—aided by the work of a variety of archeologists. She notes what we already knew: that beginning somewhere around 4000 B.C. successive waves of barbarians swept into the European and Middle Eastern areas surrounding the Mediterranean and destroyed many Bronze Age civilizations, the most important being the Minoan on Crete. By approximately 2500 B.C., the ancient world had been utterly changed—derailed, Eisler would say. Slavery, war, fortified cities, the male rule of force, religions of fear, the use of technology for destructive purposes—all of these things had been introduced into formerly harmonious, Goddess-worshiping, highly evolved cultures.

Eisler proposes two models, *partnership* and *dominator,* exquisite in their clarity, that describe two fundamentally different ways of organizing human society. The originality of her paradigm comes from the fact that she wants to include women's history in the study of human history, which, in practice, means the history of men. Eisler believes that the way the relations between men and women are structured "has a profound effect on every one of our institutions, on our values, and on the direction of our cultural evolution, particularly whether it will be peaceful or warlike."

For many millennia, communities were organized along partnership lines. People were "linked," not "ranked," in Eisler's terms. Women were respected as life-givers and priestesses, but they did not run the show: These societies were sexually egalitarian. (Eisler makes it very clear that the alternative to patriarchy is not necessarily matriarchy.) Hierarchies of dominance, on the other hand, maintained by force or the threat of force, were brought from the peripheries of the civilized world by the barbarians, here called Kurgans. It took several thousand years, but strongman rule was finally established, inaugurating what Eisler terms "a 5,000-year dominator detour." This detour quite literally turned the direction of our cultural evolution around, and it continues to determine the world as we know it today.

Not completely, of course. Neither of these systems is monolithic. The partnership societies were not structureless, leaderless, horizontally linked societies; the dominator model does not entail an absolutely pyramidal society

perpetuated by, and perpetuating, violence against people and nature. In fact, Eisler postulates that the course of history is shaped by the tensions between these two alternative systems. At some points, such as around the time of Jesus and in the Renaissance, the partnership drive is in the ascendant. At other, more frequent points, the dominator model is strongest: We're living in one of those periods now. Eisler believes that the stronger the push toward a more egalitarian, peaceful, ecologically sound society, the more strenuously the forces opposed to all that (the dominator or "androcratic" forces) reassert themselves. In the 1980s there were very strong movements for peace and social justice, for instance, and that triggered the repressive responses in Christian fundamentalist circles and among right-wingers in the government.

While this simple formulation represents ten years of work, it isn't the most difficult aspect of *The Chalice and the Blade*'s argument. The most difficult part is for Eisler to explain, first of all, why human society abandoned its pre-historical Eden for the nasty, brutish, short life offered by foreign marauders and, second of all, how contemporary society can reorganize along the lines of the partnership model.

In answering these questions about cultural transformation, Eisler gets to be slightly tough going. Not that she isn't supremely lucid at all times. It's just that the conceptual framework she uses to explain the massive systems shift from partnership to dominator is borrowed from recent theories about systems and the dynamics of change. In contrast to the linear, static models of old-fashioned science, which concentrate on the status quo, these new theories posit systems composed of self-organizing, interrelated, mutually reinforcing, mutually replicating components. Given the right set of circumstances, these systems can be upset to such a degree that their behavior becomes less and less predictable. Randomness increases until it reaches what scientists call "a critical bifurcation point" where the system has the capacity to transform itself into something completely different.

Eisler theorizes that the several millennia it took to shift from partnership society to dominator society was one such bifurcation point in human history. She also claims that we are, in the late twentieth century, on the verge of another such juncture. Humankind is faced with two drastic, diametrically opposed options: We can annihilate ourselves, or we can change our ideas. The reason why hopelessness is one of the major themes of the nuclear age is that, according to the logic of the dominator model, wars must inevitably occur. The next war will be our last, a fact that gets lost as the superpowers haggle over how many medium-range missiles to park in Europe.

Eisler proposes that we change our ideas instead. (One of the nice things about *The Chalice and the Blade* is that Eisler does not thump around like a prophet disseminating the Absolute Truth. She presents her ideas as something the reader might want to consider.) Many people have already changed their ideas—peace activists, ecologists, feminists, Gorbachev—but many more need to do so before large-scale shifts are possible.

Change *is* possible. At a given point in the past, it happened. Eisler shows how the dominators not only conquered the more peaceful communities physically, but also took the raw material of the partnership society—myths, technologies, belief systems—and transformed it to suit their radically different needs. At a definite period in the past, "knowledge became bad, birth became dirty, and death became a holy thing."

For instance, she takes the symbol of the snake. In early partnership societies it was the sign of feminine power and wisdom. Under dominator influence it became the reptile that precipitated man's fall, and it continues to be a symbol of malevolent female power, as the Medusa head and *The Witches of Eastwick* demonstrate. In this manner, *The Chalice and the Blade* offers drastic re-readings of Greek literature, Jesus, the medieval church, Marx, Freud ("a brilliant analyst of the dominator psyche, *not* the human psyche"), and Reagan's attachment to Iran (the linkage of two powerfully regressive dominator regimes).

Eisler believes that, for ideological reasons, the knowledge of our partnership past has been kept hidden or deliberately misinterpreted. In a recent interview with the *Weekly*, she said:

"We have been led to believe, in what is truly the biggest cover-up in the world, that we don't have this history—even though the clues are there. I mean, the Garden of Eden once existed. We have been led to believe that it's divinely ordained, or genetically ordained, that we live in a dominator system. . . . This knowledge, these models, I find to be very useful tools because I no longer find myself thinking there's no hope. We can only actualize our ideas if we think it's desirable and feasible—and that's the real purpose of the cover-up. Twentieth-century nihilism is a way of maintaining the dominator system."

In her talk at the International Synergy Institute in late May, Eisler stated that the three themes of *The Chalice and the Blade* are peace, partnership, and creativity. Of these three, her points on creativity are the most nebulous. Her theory is that true creativity, which she distinguishes from mere inventiveness, flourishes in partnership societies, while it is more or less suppressed in dominator societies. As exceptions, she cites the artists of the Renaissance and the Impressionists, creative in terms of their spontaneity, their joyfulness, their use of color, and their very immediate connection to nature.

The fact is, in the aesthetic realm, it's very difficult to "prove" Eisler's argument. Fortunately, Eisler intends to write three more volumes to flesh out and buttress the arguments made in *The Chalice and the Blade*.

In the meantime, read *The Chalice and the Blade*. It might make the future possible.

ABOUT THE CENTER FOR PARTNERSHIP STUDIES

Following publication of *The Chalice and the Blade,* response to the book's articulation of the partnership model as a unifying framework for our lives was immediate and catalytic. Partnership discussion groups sprang up all over the country. Letters poured in from both men and women telling how the book's new information and concepts were changing their lives.

We founded the Center for Partnership Studies (CPS) in response to this wave of interest in the book's new perspective on our past and present, and the potential for a better future offered by the partnership model. The basic purpose of CPS is to help accelerate the shift from a dominator to a partnership way of life.

Since 1987, almost wholly with volunteers, CPS has pursued this mission through publications, speakers, special events, and alliances with other organizations working toward partnership objectives such as peace, ecological balance, spirituality, and women's and human rights. At present CPS and centers for Partnership Education in regions throughout the United States work to advance the cause of partnership through two primary programs:

Education—mainly through grassroots organization but also through media and the arts.

Research—into the ancient roots and present workings of the Partnership Model in contemporary family, economic, spiritual, and political life.

CPS is a 501(c)(3) nonprofit corporation. A major source of funding for CPS is private donations, and these donations are tax deductible.

If you want more information about CPS or any of its activities, to get on its mailing list, or to make a donation, write to the Center for Partnership Studies, Box 51936, Pacific Grove, CA 93950.

General References

Abbott, Edwin. *Flatland*. New York: Dover Publications, 1952.

Aristophanes. *Lysistrata*. Edited by Jeffrey Henderson. Oxford University Press, 1987.

Beard, Mary. *Woman as a Force in History*. New York: Macmillan, 1946.

Boulding, Elise. *The Underside of History: A View of Women Through Time*. Boulder, CO: Westview Press, 1976.

Bradshaw, John. *Bradshaw on the Family*. Pompano Beach, FL: Health Communications, 1988.

Brod, Harry. *The Making of Masculinities*. Boston: Allen & Unwin, 1987.

Brown, Lester R. *State of the World 1985: A Worldwatch Institute Report on Progress Toward a Sustainable Society*. New York: Norton, 1985.

Caldicott, Helen. *Nuclear Madness*. New York: Bantam, 1980.

Capra, Fritjof. *The Turning Point*. New York: Simon & Schuster, 1982.

Carson, Rachel. *Silent Spring*. Boston: Houghton Mifflin, 1962.

Chamberlin, Roy B., and Feldman, Herman, eds. *The Dartmouth Bible*. Boston: Houghton Mifflin, 1950.

Christ, Carol P., and Plaskow, Judith, eds. *Womanspirit Rising*. San Francisco: Harper & Row, 1979.

Coltrane, Scott. "Father-Child Relationships and the Status of Women." *American Journal of Sociology,* 93 (March 1988).

Daly, Mary. *Gyn/Ecology: The Metaethics of Radical Feminism*. Boston: Beacon Press, 1978.

Fedigan, Linda Marie. *Primate Paradigms: Sex Roles and Social Bonds*. Montreal, Canada: Eden Press, 1982.

Ferguson, Marilyn. *The Aquarian Conspiracy: Personal and Social Transformation in the 1980s*. Los Angeles: Tarcher, 1980.

Fiorenza, Elisabeth Schüssler. *In Memory of Her*. New York: Crossroad, 1983.

Fisher, Roger, and Ury, William. *Getting to Yes: Negotiating Agreement Without Giving In*. Boston: Houghton Mifflin, 1981.

Fisher, Roger, and Brown, Scott. *Getting Together: Building Relationships*. Boston: Houghton Mifflin, 1988.

Fletcher, Ronald. "The Making of the Modern Family." In *The Family and Its Future,* edited by Katherine Elliott. London: J & A Churchill, 1970.

Fromm, Erich. *Escape from Freedom*. New York: Holt, Rinehart & Winston, 1941.

Gerzon, Mark. *A Choice of Heroes: The Changing Face of American Manhood*. Boston: Houghton Mifflin, 1982.

Gilligan, Carol. *In a Different Voice*. Boston: Harvard University Press, 1982.

Gilman, Charlotte Perkins. *Herland*. New York: Pantheon Books, 1979 reprint.

Gimbutas, Marija. *The Early Civilization of Europe*. Monograph for Indo-European Studies 131, University of California at Los Angeles, 1980.

——— . *The Goddesses and Gods of Old Europe*. Berkeley: University of California Press, 1982.

——— . *The Language of the Goddess*. San Francisco: Harper & Row, 1989.

Gross, Bertram. *Friendly Fascism: The New Face of Power in America*. Boston: South End Press, 1980.

Harman, Willis. *Global Mind Change*. Indianapolis: Knowledge Systems, 1988.

Hawkes, Jacquetta. *The Dawn of the Gods: Minoan and Mycenaean Origins of Greece*. New York: Random House, 1968.

Heilbroner, Robert. *The Worldly Philosophers*. New York: Simon & Schuster, 1961.

Henderson, Hazel. *The Politics of the Solar Age: Alternatives to Economics*. New York: Anchor Books, 1981.

Hussey, Edward. *The Pre-Socratics*. New York: Scribner's, 1972.

Huston, Perdita. *Third World Women Speak Out*. New York: Praeger, 1979.

Iglehart, Hallie Austin. *Womanspirit*. San Francisco: Harper & Row, 1983.

Jain, Devaki, and Bannerjee, Nirmala, eds. *Women in Poverty: Tyranny of the Household*. New Delhi: Shakti Books, 1985.

Johnson, Sonia. *From Housewife to Heretic*. New York: Anchor, 1983.

Keuls, Eva C. *The Reign of the Phallus: Sexual Politics in Ancient Athens*. New York: Harper & Row, 1985.

Keller, Mara L. "The Eleusinian Mysteries of Demeter and Persephone: Fertility, Sexuality, and Rebirth." *Journal of Feminist Studies in Religion* 4 (Spring 1988).

Kiefer, Charles F., and Senge, Peter M. *Metanoic Organizations: Experiments in Organizational Innovation*. Innovation Associates, 1982.

Kurtz, Ron. *Hakomi Therapy*. Ashland, OR: Hakomi of Ashland, 1988.

Kohn, Alfie. *No Contest: The Case Against Competition*. Boston: Houghton Mifflin, 1987.

Laszlo, Ervin. *Evolution: The Grand Synthesis*. Boston: Shambhala New Science Library, 1987.

Lebell, Sharon. *Naming Ourselves, Naming Our Children: Resolving the Last Name Dilemma*. Freedom, CA: Crossing Press, 1988.

Lewontin, R. C., Rose, and Steven, and Kamin, Leon J. *Not in Our Genes*. New York: Pantheon, 1984.

Luce, J. V. *The End of Atlantis*. London: Thames & Hudson, 1969.

Marshack, Alexander. *The Roots of Civilization*. New York: McGraw-Hill, 1972.

Marx, Karl, and Engels, Friedrich. *The Communist Manifesto*. In Robert Tucker, ed., *The Marx-Engels Reader*. New York: Norton, 1978.

McHale, John. *The Future of the Future*. New York: Ballantine, 1969.

Mellaart, James. *Catal Huyuk*. New York: McGraw-Hill, 1967.

Miller, Alice. *For Your Own Good: Hidden Cruelty in Child-Rearing and the Roots of Violence*. New York: Farrar, Straus, Giroux, 1983.

Miller, Jean Baker. *Toward a New Psychology of Women*. 2nd ed. Boston: Beacon Press, 1986.

Miller, Casey, and Swift, Kate, eds. *Words and Women*. New York: Anchor Books, 1977.

Millett, Kate. *Sexual Politics*. New York: Doubleday, 1970.

Mollenkott, Virginia. *Women, Men, and the Bible*. New York: Crossroad, 1988.

Montagu, Ashley. *The Nature of Human Aggression*. New York: Oxford University Press, 1976.

Morgan, Robin, ed., *Sisterhood Is Global: The First Anthology of Writings from the International Women's Movement*. New York: Anchor Books–Doubleday, 1984.

Neumann, Erich. *The Great Mother*. Princeton, NJ: Princeton University Press, 1955.

Noble, Vicki. *Motherpeace: A Way to the Goddess through Myth, Art, and Tarot*. San Francisco: Harper & Row, 1983.

Orwell, George. *1984*. New York: Harcourt Brace, 1949.

Pagels, Elaine. *The Gnostic Gospels*. New York: Random House, 1979.

Patai, Raphael. *The Hebrew Goddess*. New York: Arno Press, 1978.

Pietila, Hilkka. *Tomorrow Begins Today*. ICDA/ISIS Workshop in Forum 1985, Nairobi (July 10–19, 1985).

Plato. *The Republic*. Translated by Francis MacDonald Coonford. New York: Oxford University Press, 1945.

Platon, Nikolas. *Crete*. Archeologia Mundi Series. Geneva: Nagel Publishers, 1966.

Ranck, Shirley Ann. *Cakes for the Queen of Heaven*. Boston: Religious Education, Unitarian Universalist Association, 1986.

Reardon, Betty. *Sexism and the War System*. New York: Teachers College Press, 1985.

Rich, Adrienne. *Of Woman Born*. New York: Bantam Books, 1976, 1977.

Ricci, Isolina. *Mom's House, Dad's House: Making Shared Custody Work*. New York: Macmillan, 1980.

Robinson, John Mansley. *An Introduction to Early Greek Philosophers*. Boston: Houghton Mifflin, 1968.

Rockwell, Joan. *Fact in Fiction: The Use of Literature in the Systematic Study of Society*. London: Routledge & Kegan Paul, 1974.

Roszak, Betty, and Roszak, Theodore. "The Hard and the Soft." In *Masculine/Feminine*, edited by Betty Roszak and Theodore Roszak. New York: Harper Colophon Books, 1969.

Ruether, Rosemary Radford, ed. *Religion and Sexism*. New York: Touchstone, 1974.

Sahtouris, Elisabet. *Gaia*. New York: Pocket Books, 1989.

Salk, Jonas. *Anatomy of Reality*. New York: Columbia University Press, 1983.

Sappho. *Lyrics in the Original Greek*. Translated by Wilis Barnstone. New York: Anchor, 1965.

Schaef, Anne Wilson. *When Society Becomes an Addict*. San Francisco: Harper & Row, 1987.

Schneir, Miriam, ed. *Feminism: The Essential Historical Writings*. New York: Vintage Books, 1972.

Sen, Gita. *Development, Crisis, and Alternative Visions: Third World Women's Perspectives*. New Delhi, India: DAWN Secretariat, 1985.

Signell, Karen. *Wisdom of the Heart: Working with Women's Dreams*. New York: Bantam, 1990.

Sivard, Ruth. *World Military and Social Expenditures*. Washington: World Priorities, 1983.

Spender, Dale, ed., *Feminist Theorists: Three Centuries of Key Women Thinkers*. New York: Pantheon, 1983.

Spretnak, Charlene, and Capra, Fritjof. *Green Politics: The Global Promise*. Santa Fe, NM: Bear & Co, 1986.

Stanton, Elizabeth Cady. *The Woman's Bible*. Reprinted in *The Original Feminist Attack on the Bible*. Introduction by Barbara Welter. New York: Arno Press, 1974.

Starhawk. *The Spiral Dance: Rebirth of the Ancient Religion of the Goddess*. San Francisco: Harper & Row, 1979.

Steinem, Gloria. *Outrageous Acts and Everyday Rebellions*. New York: Holt, Reinhart & Winston, 1983.

Stone, Merlin. *When God Was a Woman*. New York: Harvest, 1976.

Tanner, Nancy. *On Becoming Human*. Boston: Cambridge University Press, 1981.

Taylor, G. Rattray. *Sex in History*. New York: Ballantine Books, 1954.

Theobald, Robert. *The Rapids of Change: Social Entrepreneurship in Turbulent Times*. Indianapolis, IN: Knowledge Systems, 1987.

Tobach, Ethel, and Rosof, Betty, eds. *Genes and Gender*. New York: Gordian Press, 1978.

Utain, Marsha. *Stepping Out of Chaos*. Deerfield Beach, FL: Health Communications, 1989.

Waring, Marilyn. *If Women Counted: A New Feminist Economics*. San Francisco: Harper & Row, 1988.

Wehr, Demaris. *Jung and Feminism*. Boston: Beacon Press, 1987.

Weinhold, Barry K., and Weinhold, Janae B. *Breaking Free of the Co-Dependency Trap*. Walpole, NH: Stillpoint, 1989.

Wittig, Monique. *Les Guerilleres*. Translated by David Le Vey. Boston: Beacon Press, 1985.

Riane Eisler:
Selected References

Books and Chapters in Books

The Chalice and the Blade: Our History, Our Future. San Francisco: Harper & Row, 1987. Published in German by Bertelsmann Verlag (Munich), in Finnish by Werner Soderstrom Osakeyhtio (Helsinki), in French by Laffont (Paris), in Portuguese by Imago (Rio de Janeiro), in Spanish by Editorial Cuatro Vientos (Santiago de Chile), in Great Britain and Australia by Unwin Hyman (London), and in Japan by Hosei University Press (Tokyo).

"The Gaia Tradition and the Partnership Future: An Ecofeminist Manifesto," in *Reweaving the World: The Emergence of Ecofeminism.* San Francisco: Sierra Club Books, 1990.

"Social Transformation and the Feminine: From Domination to Partnership." In *To Be a Woman: The Birth of the Conscious Feminine,* edited by Connie Zweig. Los Angeles: Tarcher, 1990.

"Cultural Evolution: Social Shifts and Phase Changes." In *The New Evolutionary Paradigm,* edited by Ervin Laszlo. London: Gordon and Breach, in press.

"Our Lost Heritage." In *Our Times*, edited by Robert Atwan. New York: St. Martin's Press, 1989.

"Reclaiming Our Goddess Heritage." In *The Goddess Re-Awakening*, edited by Shirley Nicholson. Wheaton, IL: Theosophical Publishing House, 1989.

"Population Pressure, Women's Roles, and Peace." With David Loye, "Peace and Feminist Thought: New Directions." In *World Encyclopedia of Peace,* edited by Ervin Laszlo and Yong-youl Yoo. London: Pergamon Press, 1986.

With Allie C. Hixson. *The ERA Facts and Action Guide.* Washington, D.C.: National Women's Conference Committee, 1986.

The Equal Rights Handbook: What ERA Means to Your Life, Your Rights, and the Future. New York: Avon Books, 1978.

Dissolution: No-Fault Divorce, Marriage, and the Future of Women. New York: McGraw-Hill, 1977.

Articles

"The Partnership Society." *Futures* 21 (February 1989): 13–18.

"A Manifesto for Technological Transformation." *International Synergy* 2 (June 1987): 54–63.

"Human Rights: Toward an Integrated Theory for Action." *The Human Rights Quarterly* 9 (August 1987): 287–308.

"Nairobi 1985: A Window of Hope." *The Humanist* 45 (November/December 1985): 21–23.

With David Loye. "Will Women Change the World? A Report on the UN End of the Decade for Women Conference, Nairobi, Kenya." *Futures* 17 (October 1985): 550–54.

"Population: Women's Realities, Women's Choices." *Congressional Record,* 98th Congress, 2nd session, Serial No. 98–53, pp. 167–96.

"Violence and Male Dominance: The Ticking Time Bomb." *Humanities in Society* 7 (Winter-Spring 1984): 3–18.

With David Loye. "The 'Failure' of Liberalism: A Reassessment of Ideology from a New Feminine-Masculine Perspective." *Political Psychology* 4 (1983): 375–91.

With David Loye. "The Hidden Future: A Global View from Another Paradigm." *World Futures* 19 (1983): 123–36.

With David Loye. "Childhood and the Chosen Future." *Journal of Clinical Child Psychology* 9 (1980): 102–6.

David Loye:
Selected References

The Glacier and the Flame: of Science and Moral Sensitivity. Being completed, 1990.

"The Partnership Society: Personal Practice." *Futures* 21 (February 1989): 19–23.

With Riane Eisler. "Chaos and Transformation: The Implications of Natural Scientific Nonequilibrium Theory for Social Science and Society." *Behavioral Science* 32 (1987): 53–65.

"The Human Mind and the Image of the Future." *World Futures* 23, (1987): 67–78.

"Who Murdered Peace and Prosperity?" *New Age Journal* (August 1987): 36–39.

"Moral Development and Peace." With Riane Eisler, "The Relation of Sexual Equality and Peace." In *World Encyclopedia of Peace*, edited by Ervin Laszlo and Yong-youl Yoo. London: Pergamon Press, 1986.

"The Lonesome and the Not So Lonesome Strangers: Men at the Nairobi Conference." *The Humanist* 45 (November/December 1985)

The Sphinx and the Rainbow: Brain, Mind, and Future Vision. Boulder: Shambhala New Science Library, 1983. New York: Bantam, 1984. Foreign editions include a Japanese edition (Tokyo: Saido Sha, 1985); *Gehirn, Geist und Vision: Das Potential Unseres Bervusstseine die Zukimpft Voranszusehen und Zur Gestalten* (Basel, Switzerland: Sphinx Verlag, 1985); and *Desfinx En De Regenboog: Hersenen, Geest En Toekomstvisie* (Den Haag, Netherlands: Mirananda, 1986). An Italian edition will be published in 1990 by Editzion Mediteranee (Rome, Italy).

"The Brain, the Mind, and the Future." *Technological Forecasting and Social Change* 23 (1983): 267–80.

The Knowable Future: A Psychology of Forecasting and Prophecy. New York: Wiley-Interscience, 1978.

With R. Gorney and G. Steele, "Effects of Television: An Experimental Field Study." *Journal of Communications* 27 (1977): 206–16.

The Leadership Passion: A Psychology of Ideology. San Francisco, CA: Jossey-Bass, 1977.

With Milton Rokeach. "Ideology, Belief Systems, Values, and Attitudes." *International Encyclopedia of Neurology, Psychiatry, Psychoanalysis and Psychology.* New York: Van Nostrand, 1976.

The Healing of a Nation. New York: Norton, 1971; Delta, 1972.

Acknowledgments

One of the pleasures of doing this book was that it came out of a true partnership process with many wonderful people who generously gave of their time and talent.

For providing vital experience and expertise in formulating the book's plan and working closely with us on it, we are especially grateful to Hannah Liebmann, Henry Holt, Isolina Ricci, Robin Van Doren, and Kali Furlong.

For their invaluable contributions to the section Additional Exercises and Topics for Discussion, we want to thank Karen-Elise Clay, Dorothy May Emerson, Linda Grover, Carol Haag, Ron Kurtz, Jennifer MacLeod, Arthur Melville, Harry Morel, Marsha Utain, and Gail Van Buuren.

For the artwork, which so beautifully captures the spirit of both past and present and helps tell the story of who we were, are, and can be, we thank John Mason, Jeff Helwig, Jim Beeman, and John Thompson. We also want to thank Carmen Thompson-Wilson for her counsel and helpful sketches.

For helping us work out how this book was to look, or the overall visual design for the manuscript that went to HarperSanFrancisco, we are grateful to Dan Tennenhouse and John Kavelin. The final look is the work of Arla Ertz, Lorraine Anderson, Terri Goff, Jamie Sue Brooks, and Detta Penna for whose fine work we are also most grateful.

For additional support in all the many ways that make the big difference in partnership creativity, we want to express our appreciation to Elizabeth Anastos, Elinor Artman, Michael Boblett, Emily Caperton, Jean Darragh, Shelley Jackson Denham, Nancy Ferraro, Mara Keller, Jim Kenney, Christa Landon, Karuna Licht, Valera Lyles, June Martin, Janet Morrow, Vicki Noble, Mignonette Pellegrin, Linda Pinti, Lesley Phillips, Tracey Robinson-Harris, Caty Tannehill, Jane Van Velson, and Barbara White.

Our special thanks also to our agent Ellen Levine and our editor Jan Johnson, and to Sherrin Bennett and Jeanne Gibbs for their early encouragement.

We also want to especially thank Shirley Ranck for her important input as well as for her (and the Unitarian Universalists') permission to adapt portions of the Guidelines for Leaders from *Cakes for the Queen of Heaven*.

Finally, we want to thank all those whose names are too numerous to list who have supported this endeavor both directly and through the Center for Partnership Studies.